The Reviews are in on: "So, You Want to Become a National Board Certified Teacher: Workbook & Evidence Manual"

Where was this when I needed it? I couldn't help purchasing an advance copy of this workbook—just to see what I WOULD have been able to use while I was still a candidate (I passed!). Gosh—I could have certainly used this.

Everything that the first book lacked is in this workbook. In my humble opinion, it will make the candidate's job quite a bit easier.

Unlike other workbooks costing twice as much, this little hundred-page manual covers just about everything in the required entries. Sometimes to the point of overlapping (but whose complaining?). Just a bit too late for me however.

—Dr. Elizabeth Delong

I am currently a National Board candidate and this is by far the best resource I have purchased. This has helped so much with my writing because it breaks it down by descriptive, analytical, and reflective. The workbook provides examples of each type of writing where the reader goes through and evaluates each piece. I am so glad I purchased this workbook and anyone who is a National Board candidate or a mentor should purchase this item!

—Mary Beth Freeman

The strength of this workbook is the practice it puts the candidate through. Over and over, I was forced to apply BPTS core principles to what I was writing. Time after time (ad nauseum) I was guided to 'cite student learning' and include 'I know this because...' reminders. Thank you, author, for making me work!

The charts for video entries and writing samples which the reader is 'forced' to spend hours analyzing proved to be the best help to me in the book. I was made to recognize the WHY aspect of both. As a result, my writing gleaned a focus, a purpose, a direction

More than once, I put it down and swore to not pick it up again. But I always did.

—Emri Sahad, Ed.S (California)

So, You Want to Become a National Board Certified Teacher

Workbook & Evidence Manual

Revised & Expanded QR Coded Edition

*A Candidate's and Renewal Candidate's Guide
to Successfully Passing the NBPTS Process*

Jerry L. Parks, Ed.S., NBCT

iUniverse, Inc.
Bloomington

So, You Want to Become a National Board Certified Teacher
Workbook & Evidence Manual

iUniverse books may be ordered through booksellers or by contacting:

iUniverse
1663 Liberty Drive
Bloomington, IN 47403
www.iuniverse.com
1-800-Authors (1-800-288-4677)

ISBN: 978-1-4759-3537-0 (sc)
ISBN: 978-1-4759-3538-7 (e)

Printed in the United States of America

iUniverse rev. date: 7/26/2012

Contents

Forward

In his updated workbook, Dr. Jerry Parks captures just the right combination of pertinent information regarding the National Board Certified Teacher process and practical tips for candidates.

Especially valuable are his examples, scenarios and activities that elicit candidates to analyze critically their teaching practices and how what they do in the classroom impacts student learning.

Since 2001, I have mentored hundreds of National Board Certified Teacher Candidates with achievement rates better than the national NBCT achievement rates. In working with these candidates and using the publications written by Jerry Parks, I have found his reference books to be of the highest quality and recognized by candidates as the "go to" reference book.

This 2nd edition of *"So, You Want to Become a National Board Certified Teacher: Workbook & Evidence Manual"*, includes QR links where Jerry Parks provides personal references and insightful perspectives and information for National Board Certified Teacher renewal.

Dr. Clara Carroll, NBCT, 2003

Harding University, College of Education, Assistant Dean and Chair of Graduate Studies, Director of National Board Certification graduate program

Arkansas Teachers for National Board Certification, NBPTS affiliate, Past President and Board Member

Author acknowledgements

The author would like to offer a special thanks to Lynn Hines, long-time director of the Kentucky *NBPTS* Program, with whom I had the honor to work as Kentucky *NBPTS* Regional Coordinator. Her tireless work made our program one of the finest in the nation.

I would also like to thank Carole Mullins and Marsha Reddick for their work as mentor trainers in the Kentucky *NBPTS* program, and Clara Carroll for her gracious comments, and invitations to work with candidates at Harding University in Searcy, AR.

I must also thank Dr. Clara Carroll for her gracious *Forward*, and for allowing me the distinct privilege of helping mentor her *NBPTS* candidates each year at the conference workshop in Searcy, AR. The questions, comments, and insight from her cadre helped in part to inspire this workbook revision.

Finally, I would like to express appreciation to Sharan Gwynn, whose work and suggestions regarding this workbook were especially valuable.

About the Author

Jerry Parks earned B.S., M.A., & Ed.S degrees in education from Eastern Kentucky University, and completed additional graduate work at the University of Kentucky. He became a *National Board Certified Teacher* in 2002, and has received numerous "Teacher of the Year" honors at the local, state, and national level. He is a member of the USA-TODAY *All-American Teacher Team*, and in 2009 was inducted into the *National Teachers' Hall of Fame*. He is a regular speaker at *National Middle School Association* conferences, and has served as a Regional Coordinator for the *National Board for Professional Teaching Standards* in the state of Kentucky. He is currently instructor of social studies at Georgetown Middle School in Georgetown, Kentucky,

Dr. Parks' other works include.

"So, You Want to Become a National Board Certified Teacher?"
"Mentoring the NBPTS Candidate: A Facilitator's Guide"
"Teacher Under Construction: Things I Wish I'd Known!"
"Help!, My Child is Starting Middle School!"
"With Joseph in the University of Adversity: The Mizraim Principles"

Preface to the Second Edition

It has been three years since the publication of *So, You Want to Become a National Board Certified Teacher: Workbook & Evidence Manual*.

Since the original publication, I have experienced the NBPTS renewal process, conducted innumerable conferences and workshops on NBPTS certification preparation, and dealt with more questions, suggestions and comments than I could possibly have anticipated. In those three years too, technology has advanced, and made available more diverse ways of learning, practicing, and testing, in the quest for National Board Certification.

As a result, I felt this workbook needed revision. In light of the technology advancements and suggestions made to me in the last three years, the following revisions to this workbook have been made.

1. Textual and factual errors have been corrected within the text.

2. QR (Quick Response) codes have been interspersed throughout the workbook allowing ready access to more detailed personal assistance from the author.

3. Some worktables have been revised.

4. A brief chapter regarding the NBPTS Renewal Certification process has been included.

In order to utilize the interactive QR codes, you will need a QR code reader on your phone. These may be found at the *Apple App Store* for Apple phones, and at *Google Play* for Android phones. They are free.

The QR codes look like this, are interspersed throughout this workbook, and offer firsthand timely hints, instruction, and encouragement for your pursuit of certification.

Preface

OK, you've received your 'box', and you've read the instructions. You've perused what others have had to say about the *NBPTS* process, and you've developed a plan. You're ready to go! However, if you're like most candidates, you just feel there's one thing missing before you blast off into the wonderful world of portfolio entries—how to get the whole thing organized!

So, You Want to Become a National Board Certified Teacher: Workbook & Evidence Manual is an attempt to solve this problem. Organization in writing, contexting, selecting students, and documenting are among the most difficult aspects of *NBPTS* portfolio development. But before what we discuss what this workbook *is*, let's discuss what it *isn't*.

What this book isn't: This workbook is not designed to be used as a stand-alone, easy-reading, substitute to either the *NBPTS Instruction Guide* or any other supplementary work (including this author's: *So, You Want to Become a National Board Certified Teacher?* or *Mentoring the NBPTS Candidate: A Facilitator's Guide*). In fact, this workbook, by its design, may seem somewhat random at times.

Neither is this workbook designed for prospective candidates, but rather, for candidates already in the process of developing his/her portfolio (A readiness test is included in *So, You Want to Become a National Board Certified Teacher?*).

For whom, and for what, is this workbook designed? It is designed for candidates to use along side of (not as a substitute for) *So, You Want to Become a National Board Certified Teacher?* and, to a much lesser degree, *Mentoring the NBPTS Candidate: A Facilitator's Guide*. It is also designed for workshop use. Although it is generally arranged to correspond to each portfolio entry, this workbook contains more charts and workspace than instructive textual information.

How should you utilize this workbook? Gather a supply of highlighters and pens (four-color pens are the most useful), and feel free to circle, annotate, and mark up the pages as you see fit. It is also suggested that you first make copies of various worktables (especially ones for Entries 2 & 3) where more than one worktable will be required. It may also be helpful if you work with a friend, colleague, or another candidate, but that is not necessary.

How should you not utilize the workbook? This workbook assumes you are using your *NBPTS Instruction Guide*, and therefore does not repeat your instructions. Your *NBPTS Instruction Guide* is your final word on what you must do. This workbook offers only supplementary help. Do not try to use every worktable, or fill in every box. Not everything is useful for every certification area, many worktables are rather complex, and many things overlap. Generally speaking however, everything should at least be read and considered—even if some only stimulate critical thinking about your portfolio writing, instructional context, and student selection.

How is this workbook organized? This workbook contains numerous charts (indentified as *worktables*) for you to read, consider, and fill-in as you see fit. There are also occasional *'Suggested activity'* prompts and lists given—mostly to stimulate your thinking regarding portfolio requirements. Thirdly, you will notice a few *'Timeout to refresh!'* insertions throughout the workbook. These are merely to allow you to stop and think about important aspects of your portfolio. They may seem random, but they are important to consider as you pause to refresh. Many contain repeated informational prompts. This is intentional. Such repetition is to encourage you to continually think about what the assessors will be looking for. Finally, there are numerous work pages for you to practice your writing. Due to publishing considerations, it is suggested that you also get a supplementary notebook for additional notes, writing samples, and reflections.

Finally, what's the least you need to know before you plunge into this wonderful NBPTS certification process? Remember, the charts, diagrams, writing samples, etc., contained in this workbook have been created solely for demonstration, and nothing has the official approval of the *NBPTS*. The writing samples, information, and opinions expressed in *So, You Want to Become a National Board Certified Teacher: Workbook & Evidence Manual* are not presented as representing the *NBPTS* in any way, and are solely the opinion of the author.

Also remember that:

- ❏ Sample writings in this workbook are *not* actual portfolio entries.

- ❏ Some material may not be applicable to your area, or grade level.

- ❏ Some material may simply be superfluous. It is merely presented to stimulate thinking.

- ❏ Nothing in this workbook is officially sanctioned by *NBPTS*.

- ❏ No writing sample contained in this workbook is considered 'expert' and/or appropriate writing for a '4', or what would pass according the *NBPTS*. Samples are only presented to show a distinction in writing using general *NBPTS* guidelines.

- ❏ All of the titles, places, organizations names, etc., used in this workbook are purely fictitious.

- ❏ None of the writings in this workbook are either completed entries, full-length entries, or necessarily considered appropriate in font, grammar, style, etc., by the *NBPTS*.

- ❏ Requirements for various portfolios may change over time as new certification areas are developed. Understand *your* requirements. Do not depend on this, or any other supplementary work, for accuracy. Your *NBPTS Instruction Guide*—not this or any other supplementary work—is the final authority on everything.

- ❏ Additional help can be found in Chapter 9 (Question 7 & *Final thoughts on Renewal*). While the renewal portfolio differs somewhat in its compilation, many of the same writing instructions and suggestions are very much applicable to original certification.

❑ Due to the interactive nature of this workbook, there is no discussion on the *Assessment Center* activities. There are other books (including this author's) on *Assessment Center* preparation.

Chapter 1

Introduction: The Core Propositions

Let's begin with basic stuff. Here's what the *NBPTS* expects of you. As a teacher, you should be able to evidence a solid commitment to your students. The key word here is *evidence* (note how many times it is used in this workbook!), and that's what this workbook will help you furnish. Evidence is all the assessors have to evaluate you. But more on that later. First, let's look at the *NBPTS* Core Propositions:

NBPTS Core Propositions

The Core Propositions of the *NBPTS* should be readily familiar to you. They are the heart and soul of the certification process. The *NBPTS Core Propositions* expect that accomplished teachers (teachers who perform *above and beyond* what is expected of every teacher) should be skilled in five areas listed below.

Read over all the *Core Propositions* and the prompts below. Think about them before you write. If you're working with someone, you may want to discuss these, their importance, and how you address them.

OK, let's practice as you consider *your* classroom, and how you fulfill the *NBPTS Core Propositions*. It is important that you work on this unaided by definitions from either *So, You Want to Become a National Board Certified Teacher?*, or any other book. Also, you may find there is some overlap in these definitions. An opportunity for you to do some reflective writing is provided after each proposition.

Proposition 1: *Commitment to Students*

Teachers should believe that all students can learn, regardless of background, and tailor instruction toward holistic learning by addressing multiple intelligences.

In my own words, this means:

As a teacher you must come up with ways to teach those students

I know this is important because:

Everyone comes in ready to learn.

I fulfill this in my classroom by:

Trying to reach everyone.

I might be able to improve in this area by:

More small group work.

My biggest improvement in this area in the last five years was:

Not much paper more engagment

Now, let's get specific (you'll see this word a lot in this workbook!). Be sure to answer the following prompts *clearly* and *completely*.

A. One specific example of how I address *equality* and *diversity* in my classroom is:

Clear rules on how you treat each other
Being inclusive

B. Three specific motivational techniques I use in my classroom are:

Bank
Marble Jar
Panties
Prizes

C. Describe three distinct *learning styles* of three of your past/present students:

Student 1:

Auditory

Student 2:

Visual

Student 3:

Kinesthetic

D. Three specific ways I challenge my students are:

DOK questions

E. The five most real-world lessons/concepts in my subject area that I want my students to take home with them are:

Finally, let's reflect on **Proposition 1: *Knowledge of Students***

® The three best citations of evidence I could show the *NBPTS* demonstrating my commitment to students' learning would be:

® Three ways I can become more effective in dealing with reluctant learners would be:

Find out why they are reluctant?

® My two strongest examples of utilizing multiple intelligences in my classroom would be:

_____

_____

_____

® My two areas of utilizing multiple intelligences in my classroom that need the most improvement would be:

_____

_____

_____

Proposition 2: *Knowledge of Subject*

Students must be challenged by teachers who know them holistically, understand their teaching subject matter fully, and are able to generate multiple paths toward learning.

In my own words, this means:

_____

_____

I know this is important because:

_____

_____

I fulfill this in my classroom by:

_____

_____

I might be able to improve in this area by:

_____

_____

My biggest improvement in this area in the last five years was:

_____

_____

_____

Now, let's get specific. Be sure to answer the following prompts clearly and completely.

A. My most effective technique in encouraging my students to be lifelong learners is:

_____

_____

_____

B. Three ways I make my lessons relevant to my students are:

_____

_____

_____

C. The three most important ways I utilize technology in integrating my subject matter are (remember, be specific!):

_____

_____

_____

D. Anyone walking into my classroom would recognize critical thinking skills were taking place by:

_____

_____

_____

E. Two ways I incorporate interdisciplinary learning in my classroom are:

_____

_____

_____

_____

F. Anyone walking into my classroom would recognize that it was student-centered rather than *teacher-centered* by:

_____

_____

_____

_____

Finally, let's reflect on **Proposition 2:** *Knowledge of Subject*

® The two strongest areas of teaching (for me) in my content area would be:

_____

_____

_____

® The two weakest areas of teaching (for me) in my content area would be:

_____

_____

_____

® The five aspects of my teaching this subject content area which need the most improvement are:

_____

_____

_____

_____

_____

® The most important way (outside of school) that my life experiences have contributed to my becoming a better teacher in my content area is:

_____

_____

_____

Proposition 3: *Management of Behavior*

Teachers must grow professionally, and understand how to manage, motivate, monitor, and assess students through appropriate activities, and acceptable learning goals.

In my own words, this means:

_____

_____

I know this is important because:

_____

_____

I fulfill this in my classroom by:

_____

_____

I might be able to improve in this area by:

_____

_____

My biggest improvement in this area in the last five years was:

_____

_____

Now, let's get specific. Be sure to answer the following prompts clearly and completely.

A. The three things about my classroom (besides me!) that are most student-motivating are (and why):

_____

_____

_____

B. The most difficult student I ever attempted to motivate was _____, and I was most successful in motivating him/her through:

_____

_____

_____

C. My three most effective activities in encouraging my students to take risks in my classroom are:

_____

_____

_____

D. I know these activities were successful because:

_____

_____

_____

E. Discuss your three most diverse ways to assess student knowledge:

_____

_____

_____

F. I know these are effective because:

_____

_____

_____

_____

Finally, let's reflect on **Proposition 3:** *Management of Behavior*

® My most effective motivational tool has been:

_____

_____

_____

® My three weakest aspects in utilizing the multiple intelligences are:

_____

_____

_____

® I will specifically address these aspects more fully in the future by:

_____

_____

_____

® The specific area of my assessment techniques that needs the most improvement is:

_____

_____

_____

® I will specifically address these aspects more fully in the future by:

_____

_____

_____

Proposition 4: *Professional Growth*

Teachers must make appropriate choices, interact with—and learn from— colleagues, and continually seek ways to gain more knowledge in their subject area.

In my own words, this means:

_____

_____

I know this is important because:

_____

_____

I fulfill this at my school by:

_____

_____

I might be able to improve in this area by:

_____

_____

My biggest improvement in this area in the last five years was:

_____

_____

Now, let's get specific. Be sure to answer the following prompts clearly and completely.

A. Three ways in which my colleagues might consider me a role-model of leadership might be:

_____

_____

_____

B. The last two occasions when I helped a colleague become a better teacher were when:

_____

_____

_____

C. My three specific goals (in the next 3 years) to become more knowledgeable in my subject are:

_____
_____
_____

D. If I were to be remembered for four specific ways I was an 'expert' in my subject area, they would be:

_____
_____
_____

E. My most memorable 'teachable moment', when I had to change or modify a lesson, was when:

_____
_____
_____

Finally, let's reflect on **Proposition 4: *Professional Growth***

® The most significant way I changed my teaching in the last 5 years in order to assess learning more effectively was:

_____
_____
_____

® The one area of my professional growth as an educator that needs the most improvement is:

_____
_____
_____

Proposition 5: *Community Learning*

Teachers should collaborate with other professionals, parents, and their community in addressing the holistic needs of their students.

In my own words, this means:

_____
_____

I know this is important because:

_____

_____

I fulfill this in my teaching profession by:

_____

_____

I might be able to improve in this area by:

_____

_____

My biggest improvement in this area in the last five years was:

_____

_____

Now, let's get specific. Be sure to answer the following prompts clearly and completely.

_____

_____

A. The three most effective ways (that I use regularly) to keep parents informed are:

_____

_____

_____

B. I know these ways are effective because:

_____

_____

_____

C. The last three times I integrated the community/business realm into my classroom was when:

_____

_____

_____

D. The three most important contributions I have made to the teaching profession are:

_____

_____

_____

Finally, let's reflect on **Proposition 5: *Community Learning***

® The three ways I wish I could transform my teaching into a 'community learning environment' would be:

_____

_____

_____

® The three aspects in dealing with parents I could most improve in would be:

_____

_____

_____

Timeout to refresh!

Evidence: the key to documenting everything!

You will be evaluated on the evidence of the impact on student learning you, as a teacher, can provide. Never forget—evidence—and its impact on the growth and learning of your students—is what provides the assessors with the information by which you will pass or not pass the *NBPTS* certification process.

Nevertheless, evidence of student growth and learning (improvement) can take many forms. In the following worktable are listed four forms of evidence of student learning. Be sure you address more than one form in your writing.

Worktable 1: *Evidence of Student Learning*

TYPE OF LEARNING	WHERE DID I INCLUDE THIS TYPE OF LEARNING?	WHAT DOES IT LOOK LIKE (EVIDENCE)?
Cognitive (e.g., improved test scores, homework, %-completed work, reading skills, etc.) Stress whatever success or improvements they have made		
Social (e.g., making friends, respect, positive comments, peer-interaction, class participation, teacher-interaction, e.g., asking for missed homework, etc., family interaction, etc.)		
Behavioral/Emotional (e.g., improved conduct, attendance, coming to class prepared, following directions, fewer tardies, class behavior, better respect/politeness, positive comments, accepting negative feedback, attitude improvement, adjusting to a different/more structured environment (especially important with students with learning disabilities, IEPs, autism, etc.)		
Therapeutic (e.g., improvement in some physical area)		

Suggested activity

Take your standards document and highlight in different colors the things you do <u>most</u> of the time, things you do <u>some</u> of the time, and things which you feel you <u>need to work on</u>.

Now, go through the standards document by yourself, or with a colleague, and see how well you can answer the following questions.

❏ **What are some key phrases & concepts that appear repeatedly (these are extremely important)?**

❏ **What are some things the standards mention that 'an accomplished teacher' does (see Chapter 2)?**

❏ **What are some Key 'buzzwords' that appear repeatedly (standards-based 'language')?**

Discuss your findings with a colleague or candidate.

Chapter 2

Accomplished Teaching: the Model & the Goal

You may or may not be an accomplished teacher. Nevertheless, accomplished teaching is your goal, as well as the standard of excellence by which you will be evaluated. *(See also Chapter 9, question #7.)*

In this chapter, we are going to examine what makes an 'accomplished' teacher. But first, let's get an idea of what kind of teacher *you* are—or think you are—or, maybe—the kind of teacher *others* think you are!

Complete the following prompt. Remember, you must also cite *evidence* for what you state.

"My students will remember me <u>most</u> as a teacher:

_____

_____

_____

_____

_____

Do you feel what you wrote qualifies you as 'accomplished'? Why? Why not? Did you tell <u>why</u> you felt your students would remember you this way? If you are working with a colleague or another candidate, discuss with them what you wrote, and 'accomplished teaching'. Now let's look at 'accomplished teaching'. In this way, you can identify, model, and feature accomplished teaching characteristics throughout your teaching and writing. The following descriptors are paraphrased from the excellent work: *"Enhanced Architecture of Accomplished Teaching"* (Einhorn, 2002)

Use the chart below to rate yourself (honestly) from '5' to '1' in the following Accomplished Teaching characteristics. (You might ask a colleague to rate you also!) On this scale, '1' shows rarely, and '5' shows this characteristic has been mastered.

Accomplished Teaching Characteristics	My rating
1. Accomplished teachers know their students: where they **are now**, what their students need, when their **students need** it, and how to begin taking them to that end.	
2. Accomplished teachers know how to set high, realistic, age-appropriate, yet reachable **goals** for their students, at the right *time*, and in the right *setting*.	
3. Accomplished teachers know how to implement instructional **strategies** designed to attain such goals, and how to implement such in a new or different way.	
4. Accomplished teachers know **how** and when to **evaluate** their students in light of these goals, and how to utilize students as partners in the assessment process.	
5. Accomplished teachers know how to provide meaningful and timely **feedback** to students regarding their level of accomplishment regarding these goals, and how to encourage progress.	
6. Accomplished teachers know how to **reflect** on student learning, and the **effectiveness** of instructional design.	
7. Accomplished teachers know how to evaluate what has and has not worked (and why), and **reset worthwhile goals** for student achievement. (Student needs produce *goals*, goals are *assessed*, and result in the recognition of new student *needs*.)	
8. Accomplished teachers strive to excel above and beyond the normal (typical) expectations for every teacher, and make a conscious and deliberate effort to **improve teaching and learning** for themselves, and for their students.	

How did you score? If you scored in the 'neighborhood' of 30, you're doing fine. If not, in which areas could you improve? Discuss these Accomplished Teaching characteristics (and your score) with a colleague. How do these characteristics relate to the *NBPTS Core Propositions?*

Now that you're becoming familiar with 'accomplished teaching', let's do a little reflection activity. Answer the following:

A. Looking back over your days as a student, who is the *one* teacher you would consider an *accomplished* teacher?

_____

B. What personal and professional qualities made you choose them?

_____
_____
_____
_____

C. What would you consider 5 things in your own professional life that make you *accomplished?*
1. _____
2. _____
3. _____
4. _____
5. _____

D. List 5 ways in which you strive to excel *above and beyond* the normal expectations for every teacher, and make a *conscious and deliberate* effort to improve teaching and learning for yourself, and for your students:
1. _____
2. _____
3. _____
4. _____
5. _____

E. Why do you consider these *above & beyond* normal expectations for every teacher?

_____
_____
_____
_____
_____
_____
_____

F. How do these relate to the *NBPTS Core Propositions?*

_____

_____

_____

_____

_____

Suggested activity

Be sure you continually evaluate yourself in light of Accomplished Teaching characteristics.

- Specific ways you go about determining the *needs* of your students.

- Other than summative testing, specific ways you *determine* if and how your students are reaching the goals you set for them.

- The most 'unique' *strategies* you use to help your students reach instructional goals.

- Specific ways you have utilized your students as *partners* in assessment.

- Specific '*motivating*' feedback techniques you have used with your students.

- How you *knew* these strategies and techniques were effective.

- How and why lessons you taught which you felt *were* unsuccessful—were unsuccessful, and what you did to *improve* them.

Now, let's complete another accomplished teaching evaluation. This one is a bit more in-depth than the previous one. It has been adapted from the *NBPTS Standards for Accomplished Middle Childhood/Generalist Teacher.*

Read the first column carefully before answering. Put a check in the column best describing you as a teacher. If you're working with a friend or colleague, evaluate each other and discuss your results.

Worktable 2: *Accomplished teaching self-analysis*

	Definitely	Probably	Sometimes	Rarely
1. I know the subject matter and curriculum well enough to make sound decisions about what is important for my students to learn within and across the curriculum.				
2. I know and recognize the abilities, interests, aspirations, and values of most of my students.				
3. I design my classroom to be a creative, stimulating, and 'safe' environment where students are comfortable taking intellectual risks, practicing democracy, and working collaboratively and independently.				
4. I make a conscious effort through design and modeling to help my students respect and appreciate individual and group differences.				
5. I create, select, and assess a varied and age-appropriate collection of materials, as well as utilize staff and community resources, in order to supplement my teaching and support learning.				
6. I engage my students in learning within and across all disciplines to help them understand how the subjects they study can be utilized to explore important issues in their lives and in the world around them.				
7. I understand that for each of my students there are multiple paths to learning the concepts of every school subject, and building overall understanding.				
8. I understand the strengths and weaknesses of various assessment methods, base my instruction around ongoing assessment, and encourage my students to monitor their own learning.				
9. I regularly initiate positive, interactive relationships with my students' families, and recognize them as an integral part of their child's education.				
10. I continually analyze, evaluate, reflect on, and 'fine tune' the effectiveness of my teaching, and work with colleagues to help them improve their practice as well.				

How did you do? Did you have any checks in the last column? If you had a friend evaluate you, how did their worktable compare to yours? What might be some things you could do to become more accomplished? Discuss with a colleague what you might do to address areas checked in the last two columns.

_____

_____

_____

_____

_____

Remember, 'accomplished teaching' is only one aspect of what *NBPTS* expects you to demonstrate. You must also be able to evidence these traits to the assessors through accomplished *writing*. (We'll get to that in Chapter 3.)

Suggested activity

If you are still having difficulty grasping the concept of what an accomplished teacher looks like, watch *Dead Poet's Society*, and *School of Life*. Although quite depressing, *The Emperor's Club* is also instructive. While these films in no way present perfect teaching paradigms, they do show many characteristics of highly effective teaching. Jot down as many as you can find.

Timeout to refresh!

Getting outside help

Let's do a reality check here. There are going to be times when you simply need more help and information than you have available. Numerous outside sources are listed in both *So, You Want to Become a National Board Certified Teacher?* and *Mentoring the NBPTS Candidate: A Facilitator's Guide*. Always be discriminating with any information you get outside the *NBPTS* headquarters. Remember—the *NBPTS* alone is the final authority.

Contact *NBPTS* by phone: 1-800-22TEACH

Chapter 3

Introduction to Writing: Types & Tips

Let's be honest. The most important part of achieving your certification *should be* the attributes of your teaching and your growth as a professional. While these are the essence of the certification assessment, little of this matters if your assessors cannot see the evidence of this in your writing. So, in a sense, the most important aspect of achieving your *NBPTS* certification is your *writing*. **Never forget: what you show trumps what you know! Your writing is the vehicle of communication with the assessors.**

The evidence you write about must follow the infamous 'C' words that you will hear until you are sick of them. You must write:

- ✓ *Crisply*—short, to the point sentences.
- ✓ *Clearly*—explain everything and never assume anything.
- ✓ *Concisely*—get to the point and move on. Kill the fluff.
- ✓ *Convincingly*—build an effective wall of evidence & make sure the evidence meets the standards.
- ✓ *Contextually*—put the appropriate information in the right places.
- ✓ *Consecutively*—try to follow the bullets in your writing as often as possible.
- ✓ *Completely*—answer all questions, prompts, and bullets.
- ✓ *Creatively*—not dry, dull, and disjointed. Use your voice in your writing.
- ✓ *Correctly*—proper grammar goes without saying (although, sadly, it doesn't count in the assessment).
- ✓ *Core Standards*-based—use the language of the NBPTS. Highlight key terms that appear repeatedly in your Standards book, and use them. *(See also Chapter 9, question #17.)*

As a brief aside here, you must remember that although you are not required to be a great writer in your entries, you should at minimum be an *effective* writer. While not every aspect of your portfolio writing is comprised of the descriptors below, the analytical and reflective writing should be. Effective writing is:

Accurately detailed—not hypothetical

Factual—not contrived

Insightful—not just informational

Logical—not random

Significant—not irrelevant fluff

Specific—not ambiguous

Thorough—not selective

Tightly connected—not loosely constructed

Also, remember as you write for the NBPTS assessors:

- *Showing* is stronger than telling (e.g., 'for example')
- *Information* is stronger than rhetoric (e.g., data—not theory)
- *Active* verbs are stronger than passive verbs
- *Audience* is the key (you are writing for educators not professors)

You'll get a chance to analyze effective (and non-effective) writing later in this chapter.

Also, remember that you must write about your traits as *an accomplished teacher* (Chapter 2). In other words, how you go above and beyond what is expected of every teacher. But not only do you need to *be* accomplished; you need to document in your writing *how* you do this.

Suggested activity

Your written evidence is all the assessors will have. Make sure you constantly monitor your writing with that thought in mind. Also important is that everything you do must evidence student learning, or a least, be likely to *result in* student learning. Write down on a *Post-it* note, and stick on your computer as you type: *"I know this benefitted (or was likely to benefit) student achievement because…"*

If you can't complete this statement regarding the evidence you are submitting, that evidence is weak. Understand that you must write as though you were building a case. <u>Support all statements with concrete evidence</u>.

At this point let's review the three types of writing for *NBPTS* portfolios. (See Chapter 8: 'The Writing Process!' in *So, You Want to Become a National Board Certified Teacher?* for extra help here.)

You must make sure you distinguish between the three types of writing when composing your written work. One of the leading causes of reduced scoring in the *NBPTS* certification process is a failure to distinguish between these three types of writing, and a failure to *fully* address the requirements evidenced through each type. *Describing* when you are asked to *analyze*, for example, is a shortcut to reduced scoring. **Follow your writing instructions carefully.**

Let's say it one more time: <u>writing is the heart and soul of your portfolio</u>. It is the essence of what you are sending the assessors. If you do not write reasonably well, you're in trouble.

As you should know by now, the three types of writing the *NBPTS* requires are:

Descriptive writing

Descriptive writing is your **paintbrush**, your camera. It simply *describes, lists,* or *summarizes.* Descriptive writing answers *what, when, where,* and *how, and sets the scene in your writing.* It is clear, logical, detailed and precise. Descriptive writing creates a picture. **It is concrete and observable**. Descriptive writing provides *basic information,* and *background.* What you <u>do/did</u>, <u>described</u>, or <u>displayed</u> is descriptive writing.

Critical reminder: Be absolutely certain you include enough information for the assessors to see as you see whatever you are describing.

Analytical writing

Analytical or *interpretive* writing is your **pick ax,** your **scalpel,** your **scissors** and your **hoe.** It involves breaking down, examining, comparing, contrasting, and explaining information. Analytical writing answers the *what's* of descriptive writing with *why's, how's, in what ways,* and *so what's* regarding your lesson's goals, objectives, and effectiveness. It emphasizes '*because*', and interprets or explains motive. **It is the thinking behind the teaching**. It furnishes *reasons* and demonstrates *significance.* Simply stated, analytical writing allows for the '*what it all means*' regarding your lesson, as well as how your students understand the lesson. What you <u>explain</u>, <u>reason</u>, or <u>interpret</u> is analytical writing.

Critical reminder: The '*Hemmingway Iceberg Theory'* of writing is that 15% should be descriptive, while 85% should be analytical. (This may not always be so in portfolio writing however!)

Reflective writing

Reflective writing is your **mirror.** It is your bridge to the future; your hall of modifications. Reflective writing answers the questions: 'What did *you learn* from the lesson and student work?' 'What would you *modify* or do differently if you were to do the lesson again?' Remember to include both positive and negative experiences in your reflective writing. Reflective writing is your bridge to the future, where you 'bare your soul' citing what you did—right and wrong—and tell what you would do next time. *Reflective writing is not a summary, or conclusion!* It is *self-analysis.* **It connects your role in the learning experience to the plan for change and growth.** It is simply a personal look-back on the lesson, and how you could make it better if you were doing it again. *Remember, reflection emphasizes improvement—it isn't a forum for explaining a lack of perfection.* "In light of what happened..." is reflective writing.

Critical reminder: Be sure you use concrete evidence to support statements, and include rationale for improvement. Honesty and frankness are important elements in reflective writing.

Now, before we have you practice the three types of writing, let's see if you can recognize them. This one is tough, and the correct answers are not carved in stone. A few of these are arguable, and others may overlap to some degree. Nevertheless, you should generally recognize the three types of writing here. Check the correct column. Answers are in the Appendix at the end of the book. (Don't peek!).

Worktable 3: *Recognizing the Three Types of Writing*

	Descriptive	Analytical	Reflective
1. I knew my students were having trouble when…			
2. I realized through this that…			
3. The two students were not appropriately seated…			
4. James nodded an affirmative reply…			
5. Billy's biggest writing difficulty is…			
6. I will certainly not use that delivery next time…			
7. The relevant features of my teaching…			
8. The student scores indicated…			
9. I should have corrected Thomas…			
10. I praised Amy for the response…			
11. Inconsistencies in the lesson caused Andrea…			
12. The grading scale is posted in my class…			
13. In looking back, I now understand that Amy…			
14. This activity promoted student interest because…			
15. This would have been more effective if I…			
16. The students wrote down their responses…			
17. It became apparent I was wasting time due to…			
18. The activity did not work because…			
19. I probably should reconsider…			
20. Due to the inconsistencies, I need to reexamine…			
21. I included charts and diagrams…			
22. My room has thirty-two desks			
23. In examining the data…			
24. I never got the lesson right…			
25. I will certainly not anticipate again…			
26. Lemuel was crying on the video			
27. I concentrated on proper nouns…			
28. My goal was for Tim to question the statement…			
29. I chose the series of books in order to…			
30. This allowed James to change his response…			
31. I prepared a ballot list…			

How did you do? If you missed more than 10, you need to go back and look over the characteristics of the types of writing. Now, it's your turn to practice the three types of writing. You might want to have another candidate or a colleague evaluate this.

1. **<u>Descriptive writing</u>:** In the space below, describe a concept, a specific strategy, or an activity which you have used with your students. Descriptive writing is your **paintbrush**, your **camera**.

Remember to include details. Your descriptive writing should be accurate, able to stand alone, and be clear and logical.

2. Analytical writing: In the space below, write about how effective (or ineffective) the strategy or activity you selected turned out to be. Analytical writing is your **scalpel,** your **scissors**.

Remember to include evidence. Your analytical writing should be accurate, able to stand alone, and be clear and logical.

3. <u>Reflective writing</u>: In the space below, discuss what changes you might consider in order to improve future instruction. Reflective writing is your **mirror**. It is your **hall of modifications.**

Remember to include why. Your reflective writing should be retrospective in nature, and include self-analysis—both positive and negative. Remember—this is not a summary or a conclusion.

❏ What <u>problems</u> did you experience?

❏ Which writing type was most <u>difficult</u> for you? *Why?*

❏ Now, go back to the first page of this chapter. Compare your writing to the key words. What (specifically) do you need to work on?

Now that you've actually practiced the three types of writing, let's see how well you recognize what effective writing *looks like.*

Below is a sample of two types of descriptive/analytical writing. **The sample does not address any particular portfolio entry**, but includes many examples of important aspects of portfolio writing. **The purpose is merely to contrast the two examples.** That's all.

As stated in the introduction, these are *not* actual portfolio entries. Neither are these writings sanctioned by *NBPTS*, or considered 'expert' and/or appropriate writing samples for a '4', or what might pass. They are simply presented to show a distinction in writing using general *NBPTS* guidelines. The names, organizations, titles, etc., are fictitious, and these samples should not be considered appropriate in font use, length, etc.

Let's get started. We'll begin with a general observation. First, simply read through both the *NBPTS Instruction Guide*, and the questions on the following page to get a clear idea of what to look for. Then, read the two writing samples which follow. Finally, read each a second time, and answer the following questions (be specific). If you're working with a colleague discuss both samples.

1. What makes one accomplished and the other not as good?

_____

_____

_____

2. List several ways the two scenarios differed. (Be specific)

_____

_____

_____

3. List several ways the second scenario is a better entry.

_____

_____

_____

4. Where was evidence the *National Standards* were addressed?

_____

_____

_____

5. In which entry was 'Knowledge of Students' most effective? How?

_____

_____

_____

6. Identify evidence for the three types of *NBPTS* evidence in these scenarios.

_____

_____

_____

Now, let's get down to serious analysis. As stated earlier, these two samples do not represent any particular type of writing entry for the *NBPTS* portfolio. They are merely writing samples based upon an instructional prompt. In both, the key elements (good and bad) have been underlined for you. Analyze the underlined parts of both scenarios and describe *why* you think they were cited.

You should circle, underline, note, highlight anecdote, etc., on this page. You may use your own paper if you like. Remember, this is just a writing from a prompt. Here, we're just going to see how well you recognize and analyze general writing. (Actual portfolio writing practice will come in Chapter 5).

When you have thoroughly analyzed both samples, discuss your analysis with a colleague if one is available. Then, go to the Appendix at the end of the book and look at my annotations. **Copy down key identifiers in the annotations. You will use them later.** (Note also the 'identifiers' in Chapter 5, and the 'descriptors' in Chapter 7.)

Here's the prompt:

Instructional goal: "Students will be able to describe the importance of a river system they would like to visit, and relate the importance of that water system to life in any ancient culture."

Scenario 1

In my[1] social studies class[2], the students were given time[3] to answer the prompt[4], after which I collected[5] the work. This assignment followed a movie[6] they watched[7] In Jeremy's work sample I saw[8] some difficulties right off the bat. I knew[9] he (obviously) had not understood the social studies assignment. I was hoping he would be able to relate the assignment to my instructional goals.[10] Jeremy's writing shows me[11] that he still hasn't learned to spell at a high school level,[12] that he needs more practice in learning[13] about the Nile River, and how important river systems are to cultures. I wanted[14] my students to apply their knowledge using personal examples,[15] but Jeremy got totally confused.[16] I gave the assignment again[17] and he showed improvement[18] in this geography lesson. His original difficulty could have been[19] that he's one of my collaborative students,[20] but I don't think so[21] because the rest of the students seemed to get it.[22] As a class we studied the importance of river systems, and I know my students,[23] especially Jeremy,[24] love Egypt, therefore I was not surprised many of them chose to use the Nile. Jeremy didn't seem to be discussing the Nile however, but after I talked to him, I discovered he misunderstood me,[25] and he finally got it![26]

Scenario 2

As part of our[1] semester-long study of technology in the ancient world,[2] my sophomore students were assigned[3] to answer the given prompt. They were shown a PowerPoint presentation on river systems,[4] and given an hour to complete the assignment,[5] at which time their work was turned in.[6] We[7] had previously created—as a class—a rubric[8] by which the assignment would be graded. Jeremy's work sample exhibited major problems[9], not the least of which was his grammar and spelling. I learned[10] early in the year from his father that Jeremy has always had difficulty with spelling,[11] but since Jeremy generally does better work than this—recently scoring 92% on an Egyptian essay[12] —I knew something else was wrong[13] Jeremy is a collaborative student with a severe and identified learning disability,[14] but because of his other successful work,[15] I did not believe this disability explained all of Jeremy's difficulty with this assignment. Jeremy also showed he misunderstood the prompt. <u>For example</u>[16] in prior lessons, Jeremy expressed <u>his passion for boating and fishing, as well as his love for studying ancient Egypt.</u>[17] Knowing this, <u>my hope</u>[18] was that Jeremy might relate the importance of the Nile River to survival and trade in ancient Egypt. Jeremy did indeed choose the Nile, <u>but as evidenced by his reference to "oak trees", and "the river that flows south into the gulf",</u>[19] I knew Jeremy was not describing the Nile. To be certain, I <u>conferenced with him</u>[20] about what he had described, and realized that he <u>misunderstood me to say "describe the importance of a river you have visited"</u>[21] <u>rather than</u>[22] "describe the <u>importance of a river you'd like to visit</u>".[23] On the revised assignment sheet, Jeremy <u>mentioned cities such as 'Cairo' and 'Memphis', and discussed: "…the papyrus that grows only here…"</u>[24] In addition, <u>through his reference</u>[25] to "means of transport and trade", <u>I also realized that Jeremy had made the connection</u>[26] regarding at least one aspect of the importance of river systems. From these references I knew he now understood the assignment. <u>The mistake had been mine.</u>[27] I will be sure next time to have <u>students restate the assignment</u>[28] for clarity.

Use the space below to reflect on your analysis:

After you have looked at, and copied down key identifiers in the annotations, discuss thoroughly the biggest differences between the two scenarios. Remember, *be specific and cite your evidence!*

_____

What did you find were the biggest differences between your annotations and the ones in the Appendix?

_____

Timeout to refresh!

Now, let's pause to help you think about your portfolio entries in general. You've probably considered these things, but here's a checklist—just to be sure. The following chart is to help you with your writing grammar, style, and focus. *Copy, come back to, and utilize this chart often.*

Worktable 4: *Checklist for All Portfolio Pieces*

	Yes	No
1. Am I completely answering the questions just as asked?		
2. Am I addressing misunderstandings and misconceptions of my students?		
3. Am I writing to show evidence rather than extol theories & research?		
4. Am I restating the prompts often in my writing?		
5. Am I not overemphasizing through excessive underlining and bolding?		
6. Am I taking frequent breaks to keep my writing fresh?		
7. Am I letting peers, non-teachers, and non-educators proof my work?		
8. Am I allowing my students to feel apart of the achievement of this process?		
9. Am I constantly checking spelling, grammar, font size & reading level (*Microsoft Word*)?		
10. Am I being consistent with my tenses?		
11. Am I using, or at implying, 'for example' (citing specific evidence) throughout?		
12. Am I talking *to* the assessor rather than *at* them?		
13. Am I writing as if building a case rather than as writing a dissertation?		
14. Am I writing as if I'm writing to a first-year teacher, not a professor?		
15. Am I writing clearly, understanding that all the assessor has is my writing?		
16. Am I sure I'm not going beyond the page number limitations?		
17. Am I evidencing how I grew as a teacher throughout—even from mistakes?		
18. Am I including what I might do differently next time?		
19. Am I careful regarding student names, and places?		
20. Am I avoiding synonyms, writing simply and to the point?		
21. Am I avoiding unnecessary slang, clichés, jargon and dialect?		
22. Am I utilizing my students' individual learning differenced and past experiences?		
23. Am I engaging my students in reflective thinking, allowing them to demonstrate a clear understanding of past teaching?		
24. Am I using direct quotes to/from students to show guided learning throughout the process?		
25. Am I discussing teaching strategies used, and *why* they were chosen?		
26. Is my writing insightful, logical, and does it contain appropriate information?		
27. Is my writing tightly connected and accurately detailed?		
28. Am I avoiding sweeping and unsupported generalities?		
29. Did I turn off 'widows & orphans' (*Microsoft Word*)?		

Chapter 4

Instructional Context & Planning

Now that you've gotten your feet wet with general writing tips and recognizing good and not-so-good writing, let's discuss your classroom and the lessons you will use to set up your portfolio entries. The two most important aspects of this are ***knowledge of your students***, and your ***lesson plans***. (We will discuss knowledge of students further in the Chapter 5.)

This chapter is merely a compilation of general tips, strategies, and activities you should keep in mind throughout the process. **Remember, evidencing student growth and learning is the key.**

{**NOTE:** Primary teachers, this section may be completely different for your certification.}

Before you can implement specific strategies for student learning, you must identify the instructional context of your student groupings. Here are some general questions to consider—especially in Entries 2 & 3. While some of these will be in worktables, you can never overemphasize how well you <u>know your students</u>, and how effective your lesson plan is designed to be. Think about the following questions, and how they relate to your entries.

- ✓ What is the age-range, gender and race ratio of the classroom, and how does this affect a given lesson?

- ✓ What are the students' ranges of reading levels?

- ✓ What are the unique physical features of your classroom which might affect a given lesson?

- ✓ How might the needs of the gifted/special needs students be addressed in the lesson?

- ✓ How might students with behavioral needs affect a given lesson?

- ✓ Are you choosing students representing different learning styles and challenges?

- ✓ What multicultural issues might contribute/influence a given lesson?

- ✓ What differences in the socio-economic status of your classroom make-up might influence the lesson?

- ✓ What student attitudes, groupings or cliques might influence a given lesson?

- ✓ What is the maturity level and 'personality' of your class, and how does this affect learning?

✓ What previous knowledge or prior lessons will contribute to a given lesson?

✓ Which students will most likely become 'involved' in a given lesson, and how will you address the reluctant learners? {Note: be sure to explain *why* you didn't address reluctant learners if you omit discussing them.}

✓ What other professionals will be involved or present in your classroom?

✓ What are the individual strengths and weaknesses of the students with whom you will be working?

✓ Are you providing in-depth and relevant information about the students selected for the work samples? That is, information regarding the student not only as a learner—but also as a *person?*

OK, let's get started. Here is a worktable that will serve to help plan—**and review**—lessons you will use. Feel free to make copies. As you prepare to design your lesson for each entry, keep in mind that the most familiar lesson (to you) may not be your best lesson. Sometimes familiar lessons get stale. Don't be afraid to try something new, or put a different slant on an old lesson. Also, keep your *NBPTS Instruction Guide* handy at all times. It, alone, is your final authority. Now, with knowledge of your students in mind, ask yourself the following questions.

Worktable 5: *Tips for Getting Started on Your Lessons*

Did I?	No	Yes
1. Make a list of the standards I am asked to demonstrate in each area?		
2. Read the directions completely, and compile a list of the main criteria for each entry?		
3. Take notes that briefly show I am addressing the main criteria for each entry?		
4. Look at my overall lesson plans for each of my classes for the year? (Don't pick lessons too late in the year. You will need more time to finish them than you think.)		
5. Brainstorm a possible list of lessons for each entry?		
6. Brainstorm to see which lessons best meet the criteria and standards?		
7. Narrow this list down to a few possible choices, and brainstorm with another candidate (if possible) to check for my ability to meet the criteria and standards?		
8. Come up with any new or innovative type of prompt, assessment, or activity to introduce a given lesson?		
9. Type in questions and subheadings to make sure I completely answered every part?		
10. Make sure to be specific in my writing, and not use sweeping generalities?		
11. Highlight and circle/color-code specific instructions?		
12. Make sure this lesson will have an impact on all my students' learning?		
13. Make sure to be creative in one or mores aspects of the writing?		

Effective lesson design

Now, let's get busy on actually designing a lesson. Feel free to make copies of this worktable, since you will have more than one lesson.

Effective lesson design is of primary importance in preparing for your submissions in Entries 1-3. Your lesson plan should be geared toward the standards and expectation of the *NBPTS*.

The following worktable is specifically designed to integrate both the *NBPTS* language and standards. It will take you through *planning, designing, building, tasking, assessing,* and *concluding* lessons. Most importantly, the worktable requires you to cite evidence—the key to what you are sending the assessors.

Worktable 6: *Effective Lesson Design*

Does this lesson:	Yes	No	What does it look like? (*sample evidence*)
Planning this lesson			
1. Align with the standards (Core Propositions)?			
2. Incorporate cross-curricular/interdisciplinary instruction?			
3. Evidence student learning across a range of the content?			
4. Seem to be unfamiliar enough to allow me to reflect and analyze sufficiently?			
5. Fit into my longer-range objectives/goals?			
6. Incorporate activities that reach/reflect my stated goals?			
7. Seem time-effective?			
8. Allow for student choice?			
9. Incorporate novelty & variety?			
10. Seem age-appropriate?			
11. Challenge, and incorporate higher-order and critical thinking skills across a range of disciplines?			
12. Incorporate technology/multimedia?			
13. Incorporate and utilize a variety of student backgrounds and interests?			
14. Necessitate any room logistical changes?			
15. Consider the behavior or engagement/interest of my student clientele?			
Designing the lesson			
16. Address *clearly* the expectations for students re: why this lesson is important?			

Does this lesson:	Yes	No	What does it look like? (*sample evidence*)
17. Focus on essential content (*need* to know, not simply *nice* to know)?			
18. Effectively sequence as a part of the essential content? (e.g., considers what comes before & after)			
19. Provide the structure of clearly explained instructions?			
20. Provide for student-centered activities?			
Building the lesson			
21. Build upon prior knowledge/concepts already established?			
22. Incorporate personal & relevant real-world application that my students recognize?			
23. Provide for follow-through transfer to the next lesson?			
24. Address diversity and the multiple intelligences?			
Tasking the lesson			
25. Allow for student differences?			
26. Promote risk-taking?			
27. Maintain high expectations?			
28. Provide a task/problem to be solved, dilemma resolved, or product to be created?			
29. Address relevant learning in a stimulating/motivating way?			
30. Involve cues/helps to clarify/stimulate thinking?			
Assessing the lesson			
31. Provide continual checks for understanding?			
32. Provide opportunities for (positive) feedback?			
33. Diagnose and anticipate student progress in the learning/application process?			
34. Provide for varied informational, anecdotal, as well as traditional assessment (including student assessment, and student self-assessment)?			
Concluding the lesson			
35. Provide opportunity for summary and reflection on newly learned concepts?			
36. Provide opportunity for addressing any misconceptions?			
37. Allow me, as teacher, to evidence my knowledge of my subject?			
38. Allow me, as teacher, to evidence my growth as learner?			
39. Provide substance for the lesson to follow?			

Suggested activity

To help you synthesize both your lesson planning skills and your writing skills, think about one of your classes from this, or a past year. (Assume you are writing this for the assessors.) Be specific and briefly discuss:

❏ **What were the relevant features of the teaching setting? What was an effective lesson that you taught?**

❏ **What were the goals of that lesson, and how were they assessed?**

❏ **Why were those particular goals relevant to student needs?**

❏ **Why was that lesson effective or not effective, and how do you know?**

❏ **What will you/your students remember most about that lesson?**

❏ **What changes did/would you make?**

❏ **What did the lesson tell you about you as a teacher?**

Chapter 5

Entry 1—Writing

Suggestions for Entry 1

{**NOTE:** Primary teachers, this section may be completely different for your certification.}

Now we address the most important aspect of your portfolio—your writing. Remember, no matter how good your lesson, or how wonderful your students, the writing you submit is all the assessors will have to evaluate your portfolio. How you write up everything—*not* how good a teacher you are—will determine if you pass or fail.

Be advised, this section is tough. It is detailed, tedious, often overlaps, and will become your 'death valley' experience as you work through this process. But It will give you back what you put into it. Take your time. *Work through this chapter in increments. This is the most valuable chapter in the workbook.*

As you begin the writing process, let's review a few essentials (be sure you note these):

❑ Samples of student work must show *progression* through the entry.

❑ You should include comments or feedback (for the <u>student</u>—not the assessor) on student work to show guidance through the process. Comments should relate to more than grammar and spelling. You should offer specific evaluative and meaningful praise in helping the student understand what needs correction and how he/she needs to change the writing in order to improve it.

❑ Rubrics are valuable. A rubric or grading sheet shared with the student then used for assessment is an excellent inclusion. (<u>Student-created rubrics are *especially* valuable.</u>)

❑ You must evidence give-and-take details between teacher and student.

❑ If copies (rather than originals) of student work are submitted, color copies should be sent. These will help the assessor distinguish comments from student work.

Knowledge of Students: the Core of Your Content

The key element in helping you achieve *National Board Certification* is your knowledge of your students. Every activity described and analyzed throughout the writing process should have this as the core of its focus. <u>Remember, in the writing process, you do not necessarily need to choose your brightest students</u>. Cooperation and learning improvement potential should be your primary consideration.

Now, let's do a little activity to help you focus in on the students you might select for Entry 1:

1.   Write the name of your most motivated student—Evelyn

2.   Write down the name of your weakest (academically) student—Braulio

3.   Write down the name of your least motivated (apathetic) student—Braulio

4.   Write down the name of your brightest student—~~New Kid~~ Alexander

5.   Write down the name of the student with the most discipline problems—Braulio

6.   Write down the name of the student you'd most like to see fulfill his/her abilities—Angel

7.   Write down the name of the student with the strongest support at home—Fabian

8.   Write down the name of the student with the least support at home—Angel

9.   Write down the name of the student who has improved the most recently—Jazmyn

10. Write down the name of the student who can best express his/herself in writing—Diana

11. Write down the name of the student who enjoys your class most—Lesley

12. Write down the name of the student who enjoys your class least—Braulio

As you look over this list, do you see any names appearing more than once? In this list you should probably find the names of the students you will be working with on Entry 1. Choose the four you feel would best represent you in the entry. After you've done that, rate your knowledge of each student according to the traits listed in the worktable. Give yourself a '4' for exceptional knowledge of the student, a '3' for good knowledge, a '2' for fair, a '1' for poor, and a '0' for no knowledge. Add your totals at the end. Students with less than a score of 70 or so should probably be reconsidered, allowing you to choose another student from your original four. **Rate your knowledge of the student's attributes, not your valuation of their skills and interests.**

Worktable 7: *Knowledge of Student Attributes*

How well do I know this student's:	Student 1	Student 2	Student 3	Student 4
1. Interests?				
2. Beliefs?				
3. Aspirations & goals in life?				
4. Attitudes?				
5. Values?				
6. Experiences?				
7. Learning skills?				
8. Ability to relate to real-world experiences?				
9. Special needs in particular learning areas?				
10. Socio-economic background influence?				
11. Ability to evaluate his/her self-worth and its effect on learning?				
12. Ability to respond to challenge, opportunity, & inquiry?				
13. Willingness to participate?				
14. Ability to express their responses to feedback?				
15. Ability to show improvement?				
16. Ability to relate to peers & adults?				
17. Background?				
18. Parental support?				
19. Dependability & reliability?				
20. Cooperation, enthusiasm, & behavior?				
21. Distinct learning styles & character habits?				
22. Social skills?				
23. Work ethic (time on task)?				
24. Attendance habits?				
25. Ability to express interpretive skills regarding issues and events?				

At this point you should have a fairly good idea of the two students you know well enough to feature in this entry. <u>Remember, you do not necessarily need to feature your *best* students.</u> Rather, students which can show the greatest improvements might be better choices.

OK, now let's get down to specifics. As you consider your students for Entry 1, complete the following worktable in order to help you become more knowledgeable of the two students you will be working with. (There is a more detailed worktable which follows. While that one is intended to be a post-writing reflection, it may also be used in conjunction with this matrix.)

Worktable 8: *Knowledge of Students Matrix (Entry 1)*

	Student 1	**Student 2**
1. What are this student's academic strengths, weaknesses, learning styles, etc.?		
2. What do I know about this student's physical, emotional, academic, and behavioral background that might influence this assignment?		
3. What are the interests, talents, aspirations, and goals of this student?		
4. What evidence can I cite of growth and development (mental, social, emotional, behavioral, etc.) in this student?		
5. How does this student interact with, react and respond to: adults, peers, challenges, feedback, etc.?		
6. How does this student feel about his/her own self-worth?		
7. What are the greatest needs in this student's life, and how do I know this?		
8. Why is it important that these needs be met *at this time* and *in this setting?*		
9. What are my goals for this student, and how do I ensure these goals are realistic, appropriate, and measurable?		

	Student 1	**Student 2**
10. How will I provide timely, meaningful, and appropriate feedback in measuring this student's progress throughout the process?		
11. How will I ensure that this student will have a role in the assessment process?		
12. Why are the writing themes/topics/prompts I have chosen suited to this particular student?		
13. Are there any hardships this student may have faced which might affect his/her perspective on this assignment?		
14. What are this student's perspectives on life and learning?		
15. How might this student be affected by his/her socio-economic background?		
16. What special needs might this student have?		

Having completed these worktables, you should be able to easily select your students for Entry 1. Your task is to take them through the writing process. Once your students have finished the writing process, your job is to relate to the assessors how your students made progress and how you led them through the endeavor. Remember—it's not how good a teacher you might be, or how interesting your writing challenges. ***It's how you evidence—through your writing—how you contribute to student growth as a writer.***

The following worktable is for you to cite evidence for student growth in your two students' writing. It will also help you in your *knowledge of students* requirement. You will probably want to make copies of this table so you can use one with for each student. When you have completed your Entry 1 writing samples, use the following worktable to be sure you addressed everything the *NBPTS* will be looking for. Remember, <u>evidence</u> is the key.

Worktable 9: *Student Writing Matrix*

	Writing sample 1	Writing sample 2	Writing sample 3
1. How did this student **evidence personal growth** throughout the drafting and revising process?			
2. How did this student's writing **meet the goals** I set for them?			
3. How did my feedback to this student **evidence my knowledge of their unique needs, past experiences, and interests?**			
4. How did my feedback to the student **show guidance through the writing process?**			
5. How did this student's implementation of my feedback **evidence student growth as a writer** (ability to explore ideas, acquire & organize new information, etc.) in the writing process?			
6. How did I assess this student's work throughout the writing process and how did assessment **contribute to student learning?**			

	Writing sample 1	Writing sample 2	Writing sample 3
7. **What did I learn** about this student throughout this process, and were there any misconceptions I need to readdress?			
8. What would I like to see in this **student's academic, social, behavioral, & emotional development** in the next year?			
9. What led me to **choose** this particular student?			
10. Why did I **choose for this student the particular lessons, topics, or assignments** used in this entry?			
11. What specific things did this **student do well, poorly, reluctantly,** and why?			
12. What specific feature of this **student's responses made the most impression** on me and why?			
13. What specific response might have been an **indicator of bias** due to the student's background?			

	Writing sample 1	Writing sample 2	Writing sample 3
14. What aspects of the **student's background** might the assessor need to know in order to understand a particular response?			
15. How well did the student maintain **purpose, audience awareness, voice, and proper grammar** throughout the process?			
16. What **critical moment in the writing process impacted this student** or the lesson in particular? In what way?			
17. What was one particular **insight this student featured that made me aware he/she really understood** the necessity of, & learning from, this assignment?			
18. What, if any, were ways in which this **student assisted me in the development of the rubric** for this assignment?			

	Writing sample 1	**Writing sample 2**	**Writing sample 3**
19. What were some **needs this student had as a writer**, and how did his/her writing develop through this assignment?			
20. How did these assignments help this student make a meaningful **connection to writing as a tool** for learning?			
21. How did this student show **development as a writer** throughout the stages process?			
22. What would **I do differently** if I were to use each of these assignments again with the same students? Explain fully.			
23. How did I **share both formative and summative assessment** of this assignment with the student?			
24. Did I show evidence of **give and take details** between teacher & student?			

Ok, your students have completed the requirements for Entry 1. You have their sample writing pieces. The students are finished—but your work has just begun! You are now going to utilize all the accomplished teaching intangibles you learned in Chapter 2. You are going to put into writing everyt hing you've learned about the three types of writing: descriptive, analytical, and reflective. Are you ready to roll?

The following sample will help you recognize evidence in writing as you hone your analytical skills. In Chapter 3 you practiced using a *general* writing prompt, but now we're getting closer to the real thing!

First, read through the sample. If you're working with a colleague, discuss why this is an accomplished piece (it is). *The underlined parts are the keys,* but not all you should look for. Next, in the column to the right, *analyze* why this is accomplished writing. Remember, in Entry 1 of your portfolio, it's not so much what you as a teacher actually *do* with your students that matters. ***It's what you show the assessors—through your writing—that you do.*** Some of what I'm having you do may seem simple, obvious, and routine, but the key is in having you write it up clearly for the assessors. Your writing—not your teaching skill—is the emphasis here. Remember, this is a sample only. It is not a submitted entry, and does not necessarily represent what the *NBPTS* is looking for in your writing. When you finish, discuss with another candidate, or colleague, your impressions. ***Cite your evidence—don't simply make sweeping generalities.*** After this, go to the Appendix at the end of the book and look at my annotations. **Copy down key identifiers in the annotations. Compare them with those you found in Chapter 3.** You will use the key 'identifiers' in Worktable #13. (Note, too, the 'descriptors' in Chapter 7.)

Entry 1 Writing Sample

One of Danielle's strengths in literacy-related activities <u>is that she can include detail in telling stories</u>.[1] <u>For example</u>,[2] in the fall, <u>we</u>[3] wrote personal narratives. Danielle chose to write about a time when she got to visit the auto plant with her aunt. She told me many details about her experiences at her aunt's and what happened that day with the cars.

<u>In preparation for writing</u>,[4] I planned activities <u>requiring my students</u>[5] to read a text and then answer comprehension questions. Danielle had trouble <u>analyzing text and putting it into writing</u>.[6] She tended to forget what she read and failed to answer the question <u>in her writing</u>.[7] I believe <u>this was due to the fact</u>[8] that, <u>according to her previous teachers</u>,[9] Danielle has had reading comprehension difficulties since kindergarten. To determine <u>Danielle's reading level</u>,[10] I formally tested her <u>using the Developmental Reading Assessment</u>.[11] <u>I also used informal assessments to determine</u>[12] her reading ability <u>such as tracking her accuracy</u>[13] while she orally read and analyzing her responses to reading through her writings.

The results of these various literacy activities <u>indicated to me</u>[14] that Danielle tended to begin her writing with great ideas <u>which met the goals of the writing activity</u>.[15] Yet, she has trouble thoroughly developing those ideas. <u>I knew this because she finished her writing pieces leaving insufficient details</u>[16]. <u>To help Danielle</u>,[17] I designed many "practice" activities, and <u>then assessed her ability to retell a story</u>[18] after my instruction.

After analysis of Danielle's story retelling, <u>I determined</u>[19] that she was able to give more details in her writing than she had shown in earlier assessments. I began teaching memoirs and decided to implement more specific goals into this writing activity for Danielle. The <u>results of her memoir revealed to me</u>[20] that she did grow <u>in the area of organization</u>. <u>For example</u>,[21] she was able to develop distinct paragraphs with some logical order, a lead, and a conclusion.

Chapter 6

Entries 2 & 3—Those Videos

Now we come to your videos. These should be the most enjoyable part of your portfolio entries. At least they will be for your students! The videos provide evidence which assessors use to see how you, as teacher, develop plans resulting in meaningful learning experiences for students.

In assessing your videos, scorers generally read the written commentary first and watch the video afterward. It is extremely important that the former reflect, explain, and clarify the latter. Here's what the scorers will be looking for:

- **Knowledge of Students**—Be sure your writing reflects personal knowledge of individual students, not just students as a class. This could include family background, learning style, lesson modification, interrelationship with other students and adults, etc.

- **Meeting Lesson Goals**—That is, how your goals for this lesson are relevant to the standards and the students. Remember, you must also discuss the 'why' of such relevance, as well as how <u>students</u> know such goals are relevant. Be specific!

- **Did the students 'get it'?**—And how did you know the students understood the lesson (or not)? Stress the use of questioning for assessment during the taping, as well analysis of student discussion evidenced on the videos.

- **Student engagement**—as revealed through group discussion, relevant comments, answered questions, etc. Be sure to include as many students as possible in the video.

Suggested Activity

You should video several lessons. Consider sharing your videos with a colleague or friend. Get their input on what worked and what didn't. When you have narrowed your best videos down to two or three, watch each one 4 times (yes, you will get sick of them!).

✓ *Watch each once by yourself. Take notes on the positives and negatives of each session.*

✓ *Watch each once with your students. Note all insightful comments made, and include these in your writing analysis and reflection.*

✓ *Watch each once with a friend or colleague, and solicit their input.*

✓ *Finally, watch each once silently—volume turned off. Analyze and reflect in your writing what you learned from all 4 viewings.*

OK, let's get you started with a little quiz to see how much you know about these entries. Circle **T** (true), **F** (false), or ☺ (Not a clue, but I better learn this one!) Answers are in the Appendix at the end of the book.

Pre-videotaping quiz:

1. **T F** ☺ The setting for your videos must be a classroom.

2. **T F** ☺ Teachers should talk directly to the camera as a reflecting process.

3. **T F** ☺ All students should be *clearly* seen and heard.

4. **T F** ☺ It is important for assessors to see you and your students together.

5. **T F** ☺ A quality PZM microphone is required for your video recording.

6. **T F** ☺ You may use the same students for both videos.

7. **T F** ☺ Humor is inappropriate on videos and should be edited out.

8. **T F** ☺ Assessors must be able to see a learning environment through videos.

9. **T F** ☺ Your appearance is of prime importance in the assessment.

10. **T F** ☺ A release form is required for every student seen or heard in the videos.

11. **T F** ☺ If you have a high quality video, a lack of standards addressed in a bit more acceptable.

12. **T F** ☺ How well students interact with each other is a primary concern to assessors.

13. **T F** ☺ If you edit, pause, or stop your videos, they are unscorable.

14. **T F** ☺ Scripting difficult-to-hear, or foreign language portions of the videos is not permitted

15. **T F** ☺ Teacher/student mistakes in filming generally require you to redo the video.

16. **T F** ☺ Having the students practice being before a camera generally makes a better video.

17.   **T   F**   ☺   It is helpful to allow others to view your videos for evidence of standards.

18.   **T   F**   ☺   Typical interruptions should be included for assessors to see how you handle them.

19.   **T   F**   ☺   You should always begin your tape when you begin your class.

20.   **T   F**   ☺   Assessors will stop watching your video after the specified time limit.

21.   **T   F**   ☺   You are not allowed to copy for yourself any video you mail in.

22.   **T   F**   ☺   You should restrict descriptive writing in video entries, and focus on analysis.

23.   **T   F**   ☺   Videos can be shorter—but not longer, than the allotted time

24.   **T   F**   ☺   Dates, times, names (or nametags) are not permitted in the videos.

25.   **T   F**   ☺   You cannot show students used in Entry 1.

So how did you do? If you didn't get at least 18 correct, you need to go back and brush up on your instructions for Entries 2 & 3. (I have included some helpful information in *So, You Want to Become a National Board Certified Teacher?*)

Although we've already done a worktable for *general* lesson planning (Chapter 4), let's do one specifically for your videos. As stated earlier, these tables are exhausting, repetitive, and often overlap. You're getting tired by this point, but you will get out of this effort what you put into it. In the video entries, more than in any of the others, Murphy's Law will prove to be true! Be prepared! In dealing with technology, anything that *can* go wrong *will* go wrong! Whatever happens, don't panic. You can always video again.

Be sure you understand that the videos are merely the vehicles for what *really* counts—your writing. **In your writing, the 'B' word *(because)* is your 'E' word *(evidence)*.** Before you begin Entries 2 or 3, make sure you can complete this *Lesson Preparation Matrix*. It will help you gain insight into your lessons for the videos, your students, and the context of your classroom.

Complete the following prompts:

Worktable 10: *Lesson Preparation Matrix (Entries 2 & 3)*

	ENTRY 2	ENTRY 3
1. The goals/objectives for this lesson include:		
2. I know these goals are appropriate for my students at this time **because**:		
3. The preparatory and follow-up lessons and goals included:		
4. The instructional activities, strategies, and Q&A techniques I will use in these lessons include:		
5. My **evidence** for including differentiated instruction in these lesson includes:		
6. Anticipatory concerns & distractions, and how I will address them, in this lesson might include:		
7. Multimedia, technology, and external resources to be used, and how they impact student learning include:		

	ENTRY 2	ENTRY 3
8. Modifications to my room, routine, etc., in teaching this lesson include:		
9. I will make connections to my students' interests, learning styles, and backgrounds, by:		
10. I will continually assess during this activity by:		
11. I will make, and help my students make, connections to other subject areas through:		
12. I will make real-world connections for my students through:		
13. To address higher level thinking skills, and promote high expectations I will:		
14. To assure my students take responsibility, and are held accountable for learning, I will:		
15. I will make sure my students connect to prior lesson material through:		

	ENTRY 2	ENTRY 3
16. I will make sure *all* my students are arranged in the best possible learning environment for teacher/student interaction by:		
17. I will make sure all my students are involved and actively engaged by:		
18. To make sure all my students are easily seen and heard on the videos, I:		
19. I will make sure my students are grouped (tables, desks, etc.) in the least restrictive learning environment for this lesson by:		
20. My reluctant learners are: (and I will ensure their needs are addressed and that they are learning by:)		
21. I will make sure my students are comfortable taking risks by:		
22. I will make sure my students are learning independently by:		

If you are sure everything in the worktable is addressed (and evidenced), you should do fine on these entries. Go ahead and video the lessons for Entries 2 & 3.

After you have completed your video entries, here is a *general* worktable which will allow you to cite your evidence for addressing everything the *NBPTS* wants to see on the videos. **Worktables 11 & 12 are the most thorough worktables you will find for making successful videos.** Feel free to make copies of these worktables.

Since you have many things to consider in your writing and reflecting on the videos, here's a 'time table' to help you organize as you watch your videos and identify the evidence. Mark the columns at the time sequence interval to make sure you are evidencing the rubrics.

Worktable 11: *Video Workpage*

Minute Interval Location	1-2	3-4	5-6	7-8	9-10	11-12	13-15
Student Engagement							
Use of multiple resources							
Real-world connection							
Safe risk-taking environment							
Higher level thinking questions							
Varied Assessment (including student -assessment)							
Standards addressed							
Challenging Environment							
Multiple intelligences addressed							
Differentiated goals addressed							
Probing for extended thinking							
Students responsible for independent learning							
Positive & appropriate feedback							
Teacher/student interaction							
Misconceptions addressed							
Students coming to own conclusions							

Now that you have completed your videos and a *general* worktable for evidence, here is a more thorough *reflective* worktable. Fill in the following worktable to make sure you addressed the fine details—in your videoing and in your writing—which you needed to consider in these entries. Remember, it's often the details that separate an average entry from a certifying entry.

Worktable 12: *Video Reflection Worktable (Entry 2 & 3)*

Did I:	No	Yes	What is your Evidence?
1. Check the video for **clear picture, sound, and time block?**			
2. Select any **quotes** to include and analyze in my writing?			
3. **Use varied & level-appropriate questioning** techniques?			
4. Utilize appropriate **'wait' time** on questions?			
5. Involve **all students** in the learning process?			
6. Address learning styles through **multiple intelligences?**			
7. Utilize **multiple resources?**			
8. **Make cross-curricular connections?**			
9. **Make real-world connections**, to their experiences, personal lives, and a 'bigger picture'?			
10. **Link prior learning** connections?			
11. Cite any **mistakes**, and what I would do differently the next time I taught this lesson?			
12. Make accommodations for specific student needs; **special needs**, etc.?			

Did I:	No	Yes	What is your Evidence?
13. Establish **a 'safe', risk-taking environmental** atmosphere?			
14. **Actively engage & motivate all** students, including my reluctant learners?			
15. **Manage my time** effectively.			
16. Assure students were **interacting with teacher**?			
17. Address all **IEP/504 Plan** aims, objectives, & modifications?			
18. Assure students were **interacting with peers**?			
19. Address the **NBPTS Standards**?			
20. Share my videos with a colleague or friend to get their input on **what worked…and what didn't**?			
21. Assure all my **students' faces** could be seen and heard clearly?			
22. **Restate** and **clarify** when necessary?			
23. Show in my writing the **successes** and **failures** of this lesson?			
24. Clearly show that this lesson had an **impact on all my students' learning**?			
25. Assure my students were **meeting my selected goals/ objectives**?			
26. Clearly write **what I would change** the next time I taught this lesson?			

Did I:	No	Yes	What is your Evidence?
27. Assure students were **coming to their own conclusions?**			
28. Assure my students saw **practical relevance** in this lesson?			
29. Allow **students choice**, and **decision-making** skills?			
30. Cite my evidence of **redirecting** misconceptions, misunderstood and/or difficult questions?			
31. Cite and analyze the **facial expressions** & **body language** of various students in the video?			
32. Cite and analyze if and how I sufficiently **prepared my students** for this lesson?			
33. Cite how I handled any **disruptions** and/or **distractions?**			
34. Cite evidence of **constructive feedback?**			
35. Foster rapport, and **mutual respect** for new ideas, differing opinions, respect for differences, etc.?			
36. Show student **involvement (discussion)** in learning, and what those who weren't involved were doing?			
37. Cite any unanticipated **'teachable moments'** which occurred, how they were handled, and what I learned from them?			

Did I:	No	Yes	What is your Evidence?
38. Show myself as **facilitator**, providing assistance when necessary, and not merely as the expert in the room?			
39. Show **diversity** awareness?			
40. Show **positive and appropriate feedback?**			
41. Show recognition of **students as individuals,** and demonstrate such a connection through use of students' names, feedback, eye contact, and movement?			
42. Evidence **varied, continual, effective & appropriate assessment (particularly student assessment)?** (i.e., you know they 'got it'!)			
43. Evidence **active listening** by students AND their teacher?			
44. **Promote deeper thinking, and challenge** students to reflect, compare, contrast, analyze, apply, speculate, predict, and evaluate concerning what they were learning?			
45. **Allow students to summarize/paraphrase** key points at frequent intervals in order to maintain focus?			
46. Give the assessor the impression I really enjoyed what I was doing, through **enthusiasm and energy?**			
47. **Encourage** my students in order to develop self-confidence?			

Did I:	No	Yes	What is your Evidence?
48. Evidence how I know the **students understood the necessity, importance, and real-world connection** of the lesson?			
49. Invite and encourage **problem-solving?**			
50. Evidence the students were **reasoning, discussing, and concluding?**			
51. Ensure the discourse was relevant to the lesson, and does it help students achieve instructional goals?			
52. Ensure that **differentiated learning goals** were set and met for individual students?			
53. Ensure that **independent learning** was involved?			

Before we leave Entries 2 & 3, let's give you an opportunity to analyze (there's that word again) the distinction between accomplished and less accomplished writing. You've done this before, but now you'll do it with the video entries. Go back to Chapters 3 & 5 and note the key 'identifiers' you copied down from the annotations. Use them here and in your writing. Note, too, the 'descriptors' in Chapter 7. **Again: this sample is not an actual entry, nor does it represent what the NBPTS might be looking for.** It is merely a sample for you to practice looking for distinctions between accomplished and less accomplished writing. <u>Unlike previous sample writings, there is no annotated listing of why one sample is better than the other.</u> You should be able to recognize these own your own, but if you have difficulty, go back and review Chapters 3 & 5.

Worktable 13: *Writing Analysis Comparison*

Accomplished Response	Less Accomplished Response	So, what's the difference?
I have deliberately set up my classroom in a way to encourages reading development in all learners.	My classroom encourages reading.	
In the first part of the video tape, I feature how I utilize small reading groups to enhance learning. I chose this arrangement so that students would be in a small group setting with students on similar reading levels, and with similar goals.	As you can see in the video, my students are arranged in reading groups to help facilitate learning.	
Two of my students, who are non-readers and academically/developmentally below second grade levels, are currently using independent centers during the small group instruction time to meet their individualized needs. One girl (with black curly hair in video at the green bookshelf) is visually impaired and must use a large screen to work on activities. Another student, Brent, (boy with the glasses sitting at the media center in back of room) is listening to a book about "Mr. Fraction" which integrates our math unit with reading. (I was especially encouraged by this choice, and complimented Brent on his selection, since he has shown reluctance with math!) I encourage these students to help each other, and allow each to choose between word puzzles, interactive DVDs or websites, and books on tape to enhance and improve their reading skills.	As you can also see, some of my students are not in a group but are practicing independent learning which I feel is important at this grade level. Independent learning addresses multiple intelligences and various aspects of differentiated learning goals. My students do not all function on the same level. For example, you can see that one girl is visually impaired and is using a larger screen, and the boy at the media center is utilizing listening skills (with which he has difficulty). I give such students a variety of media resources in order to enhance their learning.	

Accomplished Response	Less Accomplished Response	So, what's the difference?
Another student, Haj, (the boy nodding off in the front) I knew had been up late the night before with a sick brother, so I tried to keep him alert through complimenting him at every legitimate opportunity.	By the way, Haj, the boy nodding off in the front, does this often. This is not unusual, considering his home life.	
I prepared each student by having them complete a reading survey and describe types of subjects and characters they enjoyed reading. This survey allowed me to choose certain books for our classroom library. The students could then choose books which I color coded by reading level. I encouraged my students to check out and take home such books, in addition to using them in our reading groups. Having the access to books on their personal reading level impacted student learning by allowing my students to independently find books which they are comfortable with through checking the colored label. The Elementary Reading Jumpstart Program (ERJP) which our school has adopted has provided many leveled choices for our reading groups to choose from, and has supplied multiple copies so that strategies and skills can be taught from one common book.	To prepare my students for this event, I had each student pick out one book from our room's media library. Books are color coded by reading level to help me better know what level the students are choosing. I encouraged my students to spend a lot of time with the books so they could decide what they really enjoyed. We had a special program at our school to help select the books.	
I encourage and challenge my students to use the vocabulary ladder on my wall, frequently to add new words, and practice decoding activities as whole group and small group learning activities. I use a variety of marker boards to write on as I teach certain strategies.	As you can see from the video, I have incorporated various strategies in my room to help my students learn and decode new words.	

Accomplished Response	**Less Accomplished Response**	**So, what's the difference?**
The students featured in my group on the video are using a chapter book series, <u>Summer Adventures in the Lonesome Wood</u>, and a Venn-Diagram to assist with reading and writing activities. (We have used a pocket chart Venn diagram as whole group instruction, but this was the first time the students had used a Venn diagram on their own to compare and contrast.)	The students featured in my group on the video are using a chapter book series, <u>Summer Adventures in the Lonesome Wood</u>, and Venn-Diagrams (which the kids were used to) to assist with reading and writing activities.	
In the video, my students began by pointing out similarities and differences of their new chapter book compared to the early literacy books that they had been reading. I realized that this was very easy for them because they were each eager to share something. This was significant because I was hoping that this different type of book would motivate them since they had been showing apathy and boredom with some of the previous books.	In the video, my students began by pointing out some things they learned from their new chapter book. As you can see, this was very easy for them. I wanted the students to be self-motivated, and, as you can see, they were.	
One difference they mentioned was significant. The students had been used to seeing the level of the book posted on the title page and this new chapter book series didn't have such a post. Natasha, girl on the left with faded blue jeans, was the first to point this out. Being high achievers, these students strive to see accomplishments.	I surprised the students by not letting them know the level of the book, and some of my really sharp kids picked up on this.	
Next, we transitioned the discussion into retelling what they had read the previous night.	Next, I moved the discussion into retelling what they had read the previous night.	

Accomplished Response	Less Accomplished Response	So, what's the difference?
I began by asking the students to clarify what retelling meant. Aarianna, girl on the right with ponytail, stated that retelling was "telling in your own words what happened." Since summarizing is the same concept, I chose this as an excellent time to introduce this higher level word, because they will be using it more frequently in subsequent grades during guided reading instruction.	I thought it would be interesting for the students to tell about how the main characters were connected to our lives. I asked the students to read certain parts of the text and then summarize what the text was telling us about the character.	
As the students continued to summarize the chapter they had read at home, I promoted critical thinking about how the main characters were connected to our lives.	I know this would be a good way to get my students to really think.	
I know it is significant for the students to see practical relevance in the activity through feeling connected to the main character in order to motivate them to read more and to understand what is going on in the text. I asked the students to read certain parts of the text and then summarize what the text was telling us about the character. This strategy allowed me to check for their comprehension.	When the students were able to relate to the story to things in the story, they told me about it. It was clear they really enjoyed this activity!	

Chapter 7

Entry 4—Documented Accomplishments & Reflecting

We've come to your final entry—and often the most confusing and difficult. The Documented Accomplishments entry is the same for all areas, but the key is in doing this one right. Never forget: **less is more in Entry 4**. That is, you will likely be more successful including *fewer* accomplishments with more cogent detail than a large number of accomplishments intended to impress. Also, remember that the focus here is on:

- Parent interaction and family involvement (within the last year)

- Community involvement (within the last year)

- Professional growth—teacher as learner, leader, collaborator (within the last 5 years)

The evidence must clear, convincing, and consistent, and be student-learning centered. While student learning is key throughout your portfolio, *evidencing* student learning in this entry is not always easy. So keep in mind if you can't evident *measureable* student learning, you must at least evidence what might be likely to *result* in student learning. Fall back on that sparingly however. Measurable student achievement trumps 'likely to result in' every time. It's just that evidencing such in Entry 4 is often difficult. Regardless, in this entry—as in all your entries—don't offer sweeping generalities that you cannot support with evidence.

Before we go any further, here is a list of *NBPTS* descriptors that you should utilize (and document in your writing) in your teaching. Note too the 'identifiers' in Chapters 3 & 5. Remember it's not just the things you do as a teacher, it's *how* you describe them. In your writing, keep these descriptors ever before you as you write about your teaching.

'enthusiasm' in delivery
'effectively' impacting students
'skillfully' implemented lessons
'thoughtfully 'chosen strategies
'appropriately' chosen activities
'engaging' in parent participation
'substantive' in teaching methodology
'leadership' in strengthening the profession
'highly interactive' with families and community
'conscious and deliberate' in professional development
'positive change' in effecting educational policy/instructional practice
'rich, detailed, coherent' in documenting how you made a difference in education

Let's get you started with a little Entry 4 quiz to see how much you know about this entry. Circle T (true), F (false), or ☺ (Not a clue, but I better learn this one!) Answers are in the Appendix at the end of the book.

Documented Accomplishment Entry 4 quiz:

1. **T F** ☺ Surveys, questionnaires, and student contracts can make good entries.

2. **T F** ☺ A "Teacher of the Year" award is an excellent inclusion.

3. **T F** ☺ Including several Verification Forms makes things look more legit.

4. **T F** ☺ Evidence must show that you *meet*—not just recognize—student needs.

5. **T F** ☺ At least one Verification Form is required.

6. **T F** ☺ Fewer accomplishments, written in detail, are better than including several.

7. **T F** ☺ Emails and phone logs are good inclusions.

8. **T F** ☺ Student letters are excellent inclusions.

9. **T F** ☺ Community involvement must be within the last 5 years.

10. **T F** ☺ State test scores make a good inclusion.

11. **T F** ☺ Photos are not permitted in this entry.

12. **T F** ☺ A personal reflection journal makes a good entry.

13. **T F** ☺ The score weighting in Entry 4 is the same as in the other entries.

14. **T F** ☺ Professional growth must be within the last 5 years.

15. **T F** ☺ About 5-7 'accomplishments' is all you should try to document..

Did you score well? You probably should have known at least 10 of these. Consider from the quiz what things you might use in your Entry 4.

It is important to keep your *personal accomplishments* discussion to a minimum. As Richard Wedig, *NBCT*, notes: "'Teacher of the Year' accolades, advanced degrees, extracurricular activity sponsorship, and personal travel are not in themselves, the best choices for entries." In addition, some entries may overlap, e.g., you may focus an accomplishment on what you do as a learner/collaborator, or how you involve parents as a part of the community. If you use dual entries, be sure you explain the particular *focus*.

Do not allow yourself to get too stressed out about this entry. Generally, Entry 4 is the most troublesome to organize. The key is to remember to focus on entries that directly 'touch the students' first. That is, entries which best evidence how you recognized and understood individual students' strengths, weaknesses and needs. Such entries will always carry more weight.

The following worktable will give you a *general*, overall scope to what the *NBPTS* is looking for, in Entry 4. This is a good worktable to get you started. You'll see a more detailed worktable later.

Worktable 14: *Documented Accomplishments Matrix*

(You should have evidences from all 3 categories)

Category	Activity	Significance	Impact on Student Learning	Documentation
What accomplishments can best evidence: (Evidence must be intentional, conscious, and deliberate.)	What activity in your teaching context will best evidence a clear, convincing, and consistent impact (or likely impact) on student learning?	How does this activity go above and beyond what is routine for the average teacher and what was its effect on the holistic learning environment?	How do you know this accomplishment resulted in an impact on student learning, fostered student responsibility, and/or met a student need? (Be specific.)	What documentation can you furnish to evidence your participation or involvement in this accomplishment or activity (teacher as continual learner)?
How you regularly and continually worked as partner with parents, other family members, and the community where your students live.				
How you served as a leader, collaborator, and/or professional development provider to staff members and other professionals.				
How you grew and progressed as a learner in the professional development process.				

If you filled in the twelve boxes with solid, useable, and relevant information, you should have no trouble with this entry.

Now, let's focus in more precisely on exactly what the *NBPTS* is looking for. Choose 5-7 accomplishments. Place each one within the framework of the following worktable. (You may want to make copies of the table for <u>each</u> accomplishment.) If it holds up to most of the questions, it's probably a winner. If it falters, **do not use it**. Test each accomplishment as you prepare Entry 4. Some questions are general, some are specific. Some ask for evidence; for some, only a brief response is necessary. Bottom line however, you should look at the worktable as you consider each and all of your possible inclusions for Documented Accomplishments.

Worktable 15: *Reflecting on My Documented Accomplishments*

KEY QUESTION	*Evidence/Thoughts*
1. What is the significance and impact of this accomplishment? (Why is it important?)	
2. Did this accomplishment occur in the last 5 years?	
3. Does the accomplishment reflect the *NBPTS* Standards?	
4. How does the accomplishment impact your students, influence student learning, and how can these outcomes—with specific examples— be demonstrated—in the writing?	
5. How do you know this accomplishment was successful in its impact on student learning? Is there a clear connection in the writing?	
6. Does this accomplishment reflect how you *recognized* and *met a* student need? (It is important for you to meet the student needs—not just recognize them!)	
7. Do you have an accomplishment for each area of Entry 4?	
8. Is there documentation that your work with parents occurred this year?	
9. Does interaction with parents include two-way communication?	
10. Are there any accomplishments which might better be clustered and written about as one accomplishment?	
11. Does the accomplishment reflect how you are going 'above and beyond' what is expected of every teacher, or is it routine and required?	

KEY QUESTION	*Evidence/Thoughts*
12. Do accomplishments indicate your growth in professional development, and/or improvement in the teaching practice?	
13. Do you reflect upon the patterns in your accomplishments, and how your future as a teacher might be impacted?	
14. Does your accomplishment contribute to the advancement of your colleagues and/or the education profession in general? How?	
15. The most student-related aspects of this accomplishment are:	
16. Are all three areas of this entry fully represented?	
17. Do these accomplishments 'touch the students' first? That is, do they evidence how you recognized and understood individual students' strengths, weaknesses and needs?	

Whatever you choose to include, make sure your evidence is *clear, convincing, and consistent,* is student-centered in the writing, and that it resulted in—or was *likely to* result in—student learning.

Now, let's concentrate on the most difficult categories of Entry 4. We'll put aside your involvement with parents, other family members, and the community for the time being and focus on how *you*, as an educator, evidence professional growth as *leader, learner,* and *collaborator.* (More detailed suggestions on how you partner with parents and the community may be found in *So, You Want to Become a National Board Certified Teacher?*) Remember, this evidence must be **clear and specific**. Look at the following chart. Match the professional growth with the evidence. If possible, cite how you met or might specifically meet this area for professional growth. Some accomplishments may fit in more than one column, but this will give you an idea on how to evidence for the assessors your growth as a professional. When you finish, if you're working with a colleague, discuss your answers.

Worktable 16: *Documented Accomplishments – Professional Growth*
(Note: You should have evidences from all 3 categories: leader, learner, and collaborator.)

What does evidence look like? *ACTIVITY:*	**AREAS OF PROFESSIONAL GROWTH**				
	Learn from, and seek advice from others	*Study to be informed & grow professionally*	*Teach others as a way to give back to the profession*	*Reflect on what works and doesn't work in your field*	*Interact and share info with your peers*
1. Presenting sessions at national conferences					
2. Collaborating with colleagues to create unit lesson plans					
3. Keeping a personal reflective journal					
4. Taking classes at a local college					
5. Attending a session at a national conference					
6. Accepting student teachers					
7. Trying new twists on classroom lessons to see if it works					
8. Writing articles for a magazine, journal, or textbook section					
9. Leading at a local in-service					
10. Reading professional journals					
11. Seeking a teacher mentor					
12. Studying best practices in the teaching profession					

What does evidence look like? *ACTIVITY:*	*Learn from, and seek advice from others*	*Study to be informed & grow professionally*	*Teach others as a way to give back to the profession*	*Reflect on what works and doesn't work in your field*	*Interact and share info with your peers*
13. Visiting other teachers' classrooms					
14. Staying up-to-date regarding technology use					
15. Enhancing your schools professional growth & culture					
16. Peer coaching new teachers					
17. Being a model of lifelong learning to your students					

Suggested Activity

Be sure to also incorporate specific evidence for your accomplishments regarding parent/ family, community, and professional development involvement. Below are some things for you to consider in order to help meet the requirements for this aspect of Entry 4.

NOTE: Evidence may come from outside your content area of certification—just be sure to *tie it in.*

Continual two-way communication/interaction such as:

- o   *Improvement letters*
- o   *Web pages*
- o   *Class websites (e.g., sites.google.com/site/jparks7gms)*
- o   *Email correspondence (parent email list)*
- o   *Parent Facebook page*
- o   *Class newsletters*
- o   *Remind101.com assignment reminders*
- o   *Communication logs with parents/community (write these up—don't just mention)*
- o   *Surveys*

Seeking to help non-English speaking students through:

- o *Learning more about their culture*
- o *Seeking more information regarding their background*
- o *Becoming familiar with their home life*
- o *Taking an interest in their language history*
- o *Helping improve translation of learning/homework materials*

Other possible inclusion ideas:

- o *Collaboration with students' past teachers*
- o *Letters from parents, or letters you sent home*
- o *Professional articles you authored*
- o *Syllabi for professional development classes you taught*
- o *Grant proposals you have written*
- o *Inviting parents to participate in school functions, fairs, celebrations, etc.*
- o *Organizing students in community volunteer programs*
- o *Assisting students with scholarships, merit awards, etc.*

After you have selected the Documented Accomplishments which best meet the *NBPTS* criteria, you will need to write them up. Remember, writing is the key! You're probably sick of the practice writing at this point, but you cannot practice too much in honing your writing skills for the *NBPTS* entries.

Here, you will annotate another written sample. In this case, it is a *Documented Accomplishment* sample. This is neither an actual entry nor an entry deemed 'highly acceptable' by the *NBPTS*.

First, read through this writing sample. If you are working with a colleague, discuss why you feel it is accomplished, or not so accomplished. Then, begin your annotation. As in earlier samples, the underlined items are the key (but not the only) evidence. Annotate in the space provided at the right. <u>I did not include an annotated listing for this piece.</u> You should be able to recognize these own your own. If you have difficulty, go back to the chapter on accomplished writing.

Accomplishment #2

This accomplishment is a "<u>Teacher of the Year</u>" award <u>I was honored</u> to receive in 2008. It was presented to me by my county, in a ceremony at the end of the school year. <u>I was nominated</u> from among over a hundred teachers. This is evidence <u>of my going above and beyond as teacher,</u> since <u>only a few teachers receive such an award</u>. This award <u>comprises all I am as a teacher,</u> and reflects clear, continuous growth over the many years <u>this honor was earned.</u> It shows that professionals believe my <u>teaching methods are successful,</u> and that I am respected among the families, parents, and colleagues I work with. <u>I have always put my students first,</u> and tried to be a professional role-model to younger teachers. I feel this award <u>reflects my success</u> in this area. <u>Since I have taught for many years,</u> I know my growth as a teacher has been a long and learning process, and I will continue to grow professionally until the end of my career.

Portfolio Final Reflection

You've finished your entries. You're going to tie-up your portfolio with a Summative Reflection.

Let's do one more annotation. Look at the Summative Reflection below and analyze it. Using all you've learned, discuss why you feel it *is* or is *not* accomplished writing. (This one's tough!) I won't tell you which one it is—you should know. <u>I'm not underling any key word or phrases</u> – you're completely on your own! **Remember, this is a fictitious sample only. It is not a submitted entry, and does not represent what the *NBPTS* is looking for in your writing.** Discuss with another candidate, or a colleague, your impressions. ***Cite evidence!***

Summative reflection

As I reflect upon these accomplishments, I see myself as a more giving teacher, rather than just a teacher who gives. Being a teacher has become a lifestyle, where once, it was merely a job. I have learned how much more important it is to leave a memory in my students' minds than a mark.

In these last years, I attended professional conferences such as ATRW in order to interact with, and share with new teachers what I've learned. I also am much more willing to ask a colleague for help in my classroom— something I would not have done as a younger teacher. I have learned to be the best teacher I can be. I am going continue to fine-tune my skills through attending regular, ongoing seminars such as the NTYP, and various writing portfolio workshops.

Outside the classroom, the most effective influence on student learning has been my two conferences attended. My second most effective influence on student learning was this year when I challenged my school board in their decision to eliminate summer school in my county.

If I had the opportunity to change or re-do something again, I can think of two things. First, I would never have left teaching for those five years I went into marketing. Second, I would have accepted student teachers sooner.

In summary, to see the chosen accomplishment as a unity, I realize now that I love to learn as much as I love to teach, and the former only improves the latter. In retrospect however, I feel my work with students' families is the most improved area of my development as a teacher. I once saw parents as adversarial, and to be avoided. Today, I realize how willing to help me they *really* are, and how appreciative they are when I send home that *'Good Student'* letter.

And so, I have finished. It has made me more cognizant of what I should be doing that I don't, and for that, I'm grateful. But much of what was required for this process, I have been doing for a long time. Now, I'll try to do them better.

Chapter 8

Packing the Box & Final Considerations

This last worktable will be your favorite, because it's the last one you will do! Before you send the beloved box back to the *NBPTS*, check to be sure you have tied up all the loose ends. Remember though, your entries are never 'finished', just done. At some point, you must let it go.

Worktable 17: *Packing the Box*

		Yes	No
1.	Did I follow the *NBPTS* rules about student names, barcode ID numbers, fonts, margins, pagination, etc.?		
2.	Did I enlarge (200%) my photo ID and put it on the correct form?		
3.	Did I include my classroom layout?		
4.	Did I include all required forms including attestation, Contextual Information and Candidate Final Inventory sheets? (Remember—you do not have to submit Adult and Student Release forms, but you must get them signed anyway, and should file them.)		
5.	Did I make the appropriate distinction in my writing between *analyzation, description, & reflection?*		
6.	Did I make sure my *ID number, date,* and *signature* are on everything applicable?		
7.	Did I punch out the tabs on the videotapes, rewind them, and put on the *correct* label?		
8.	Did I pack videos in plastic cases for protection in transport?		
9.	Did I check the Candidate Final Inventory for each entry?		

	Yes	No
10. Did I check student work samples against the description in the written commentary to make sure I referred to the correct student?		
11. Did I omit last names and school locale references?		
12. Did I put my candidate ID barcode on each entry coversheet, envelope, and on the portfolio box?		
13. Did I make final copies of everything—student work, videotapes, computer disks, entries, etc.? (Be sure to make a duplicate copy of your portfolio when it is completed, since you do not get your portfolio back when the process is over.)		
14. Did I spell-check everything several times?		
15. Did I answer all parts of every question?		
16. Did I make sure all videos could be seen and heard sufficiently?		
17. Did I document student work samples with identifiers ("Student A", "Student B")?		
18. Did I double-check to be sure I referred to the correct student in the writing description and analysis?		
19. Did I pack the box securely, and with filling material?		

Chapter 9

The NBPTS Renewal Certification
Process—a Personal Reflection...

If you are considering NBPTS Renewal Certification, I have taken much of the information below from the NBPTS website and integrated my own personal reflections on the process. Of course, you must check with the NBPTS for all final decisions on relevant instructions, and for all updated/content-specific information at: **www.nbpts.org/for_nbcts/certification_renewal,** **or contact the *NBPTS* by phone: 1-800-22TEACH**

1. What is NBPTS Certification Renewal?

Your National Board Certification is issued for a period of 10 years, at which point you must complete the Profile of Professional Growth prior to the expiration date of your certificate. You may only renew certification in your original certificate area. You must begin at the latest in your ninth year of certification but you may formally begin work on the Profile of Professional Growth as early as year eight of your certification period. It is best not to wait until the last year of eligibility to attempt your renewal. Should you not earn the renewal, there would remain no further opportunity to do so. I felt the process was less difficult—but no less stringent—than the original certification. Bottom line, the NBPTS wants you to evidence how you have grown as a professional educator.

2. Should you seek Renewal Certification?

Unless you have a good reason not to—such as retirement in the next couple of years—probably. The process does remind you of what's important as a teacher, and does provide an opportunity for you to refocus on student learning.

3. What is the basis of the Profile of Professional Growth
for renewal of National Board Certification?

Your accomplishments throughout the life of your certificate reflect an inherent desire to be involved in professional growth to increase impact on student learning. The professional growth activities include development of certificate-specific content knowledge and pedagogical and technological skills obtained through workshops, courses, and readings of the latest professional literature. The

Profile of Professional Growth is designed to promote continued professional involvement in a variety of areas consistent with the high and rigorous standards that certification represents.

4. What does the Profile of Professional Growth look like?

Although the Profile of Professional Growth (PPG) is separated into three components, its impact must be viewed as a single entity. Things you might want to consider would be workshops, conferences, courses you've taken, your reading of and contributions to professional literature, training of other educators such as student teachers, etc. The inclusions in your PPG must be varied and multifaceted. Your PPG is rooted in:

- The Five Core Propositions and the Standards

- The Architecture of Accomplished Teaching

It has been designed so that you can show the connections you make between continued professional growth and student learning:

Component 1 requires submission of responses to prompts related to four areas of professional growth that you choose, which may have begun before certification, but have evolved to become the focus of professional growth since certification. These professional growth experiences include current **content knowledge** and pedagogy, acquisition of effective and appropriate use of **technology**, and must be ongoing, varied and multi-faceted. They must reflect your continuous commitment and contributions to the professional activities that ultimately have an impact on student learning.

Component 2 requires you to choose **one** of the professional growth experiences featured in Component 1 and demonstrate its application. This component requires a 10-minute video in which you demonstrate classroom teaching in the same content and developmental level as your original certification. It must be created as part of the PGE component of your renewal process for National Board Certification. The video and accompanying written commentary must **demonstrate student learning** in an environment that ensures *equity of access*, promotes an *appreciation of diversity*, and demonstrates certificate-specific *content knowledge*.

Component 3 requires you to choose one of the **remaining** *Professional Growth Experiences* from Component 1 and **demonstrate its application**. This component offers several options, including the choice of featuring work with students or with professional colleagues. The basis for this component must be a different professional growth experience from that used in Component 2 and must demonstrate either a direct or an indirect impact on student learning.

The final section is **Reflection** in which you analyze the connections and patterns among all three components of your Profile from the perspective of the role of an educator. Here you focus on challenges encountered, and discuss plans for continued professional growth and efforts to impact student learning. I thought this component was a bit difficult. There is limited space allowed to address quite a bit of information. Don't take this one lightly.

5. How does renewal differ from my initial certification?

The process for renewal of National Board Certification is different from the initial certification process in several ways.

- The renewal instrument has several interrelated components rather than entries and exercises that are <u>independent of each other</u>. Renewal is a 'package deal'.

- There is no Assessment Center test to worry about.

- Due to the interrelated components of the renewal instrument, a holistic scoring approach is used. That is, a single decision to renew or not renew is made based on the entire body of evidence—not individual entries as in your original certification.

- Renewal is not as lengthy a process as the original certification process, however, it is still rigorous. It took me about half the time I spent on my original certification.

- Renewal candidates will receive either a "Renewed" or "Not Renewed" decision. The reports of renewal decisions will be different as will the resubmission process for renewal candidates who receive a "Not Renewed" decision.

6. What is the evaluation rubric for renewal?

The language of the evaluation rubric is identical for all candidates seeking renewal status regardless of certificate area.

The renewal rubric governs the type of evidence that the evaluators will look for in each renewal candidate's submission. The rubric has two levels - renewed and not renewed.

Renewed:

The renewal candidate has provided sufficient evidence of the identification of important needs in his or her professional context; of professional growth in areas which address those needs in a variety of rich and powerful contexts, including areas of content and/or pedagogical knowledge; and has provided sufficient evidence of the application of professional growth in ways that have a meaningful impact on student learning. The renewal candidate has provided sufficient evidence of the acquisition of knowledge of current technology and/or effective and appropriate incorporation of technology into teaching and learning; and has drawn on and/or contributed to the resources of the school, district and/or community. The candidate has provided evidence of teaching practice in his or her certificate-specific area in ways that recognize the needs of students, ensure equity of access and promote appreciation of diversity, and provide relevant and meaningful instruction for students. The candidate has provided evidence of professional growth that has evolved since certification and is varied and/or multifaceted. Although there may be unevenness in the level of evidence of professional growth presented, overall, there is sufficient evidence of professional growth since certification to support renewal of certification.

Not Renewed:

> *The renewal candidate may have provided insufficient evidence of the identification of important needs in his or her professional context; or insufficient evidence of professional growth in areas to address those needs, or the professional growth activities may not exhibit variety or depth. The application of PGEs may not have impacted student learning either directly or indirectly. The candidate may not have demonstrated the acquisition of knowledge of current technology and/or has incorporated technology into teaching and learning areas in trivial or inappropriate ways, or not at all. The renewal candidate may not have drawn on and/or contributed to resources of the school, district and/or community. The candidate may not have demonstrated teaching practice in his or her certificate-specific area in ways that recognize the needs of students, or may have done little to ensure equity of access, or promote appreciation of diversity, or may have provided irrelevant or meaningless instruction for students. The candidate may not have provided evidence of professional growth that has evolved since certification; professional growth may not be varied and/or multifaceted. There may be some examples of professional growth experiences or teaching practice that indicate some degree of growth, but overall there is insufficient evidence of professional growth since certification to support renewal of certification.*

7. What are the key aspects I should focus on (each of which is part of the holistic rubric)?

- *Identification and addressing of needs.* That is, needs of yourself as a professional educator, those you have taught—including students, prospective teachers, and colleagues, those you have worked with professionally—such as parents, community leaders, and university professors, and those you have instructed through workshops, books, etc. The key is how did you *recognize* the need, how did you *address* the need, how do you know you were *successful* in meeting the need, and where do you go from there?

- *Acquisition or deepening of content/pedagogical knowledge.* That is, how can you <u>demonstrate</u> you are a more *knowledgeable* educator in your content area? (One-time professional development seminars might not fill the bill here. Patterns of growth are best.)

- *Acquisition and/or effective and appropriate use of current technology.* This is the easiest part in my opinion. So much technology has changed in ten years, and educators are virtually forced to keep up. (Use of <u>available</u> technology is an important phrase to remember.)

- *Involvement of others.* As with your original certification, you must demonstrate how you have involved others (community, colleagues, parents) in the education process.

- *Demonstration of standards-based relevant and meaningful instruction*. This is your video. Pretty much similar to the classroom video in your original certification. ('Standards-based, meaningful, and relevant instruction' is the key here.)

- *Equity of access and appreciation of diversity.* Also to be shown in the video and anything you write concerning your students.

- *Impact on student learning*. This is the heart and soul of your renewal. I don't need to elaborate here.

8. What is the process used in the evaluation of Renewal?

Two evaluators independently read your submission, collecting evidence for each of the above aspects as they go. <u>Each aspect does not have to be demonstrated in every professional growth experience or in every component</u>, but be sure they are fully addressed. They then discuss the submission, the evidence for each of the eight aspects, and come to a joint holistic decision. In the instance when the evaluators agree on a "Not Renewed" decision, a trainer further reviews the evidence.

9. What if I received a "Not Renewed" decision?

If you receive a "Not Renewed" decision, you will also receive recommendations for focus generated as part of the evaluation process to guide your resubmission of a renewal response. <u>These recommendations will be specific to your submission</u> but are of a standardized nature based on the evaluation rubric. (Remember, in the original certification process we did not receive any feedback about our submission.)

There will be two concerns addressed in the decision letter for candidates who do not renew. The first will identify whether there were any **major omissions** that resulted in the "Not Renewed" decision. A major omission would include missing evidence such as failure to submit evidence for any of the three components, or to omit a major part such as video, learner work or commentary. Additionally, the students featured in Component 2 must be in the age range for the certificate in which the renewal candidate originally certified, and the content focus of the lesson must be from the original certificate area and created as part of the PGE component of your renewal process for National Board Certification. Failure to meet this requirement will result in an automatic "Not Renewed" decision.

The second concern addressed in the "Not Renewed" decision letter is a list of the key aspects identified in the rubric and an indication of **whether there was an appropriate level of evidence**, or if the level of evidence for this particular area needs to be strengthened. If a candidate receives a "Not Renewed" decision, he or she should re-read his or her submission along with the rubric, and the decision letter indicating the areas identified as in need of strengthening. For areas where the level of evidence is in need of strengthening, the candidate should consider whether there are alternative professional growth experiences that would provide richer evidence.

10. When should I apply for renewal?

You may begin the process as early as the eighth year of certification to ensure adequate time to successfully complete the renewal process. I would not recommend waiting until the last eligible year.

11. What are the requirements for renewal?

• Your original 10-year certificate must be valid when you apply for renewal.

• You must be at the end of your eighth, in your ninth, or at the beginning of your tenth year of certification to begin the renewal process. NBCTs whose certification has expired are not eligible for renewal.

• Your state teaching license must be current and unencumbered (e.g. not suspended or revoked). Teachers who are not required by the state to hold a license must submit proof that the school in which they teach is recognized and approved to operate by the state. Renewal candidates who are not actively teaching but plan to establish a relationship and work with students of a colleague in order to complete renewal must meet the teaching licensure requirements of the state.

12. What is the fee for renewal?

The total current fee for certificate renewal is $1,150, which includes a $300 non-refundable application fee. <u>This fee is subject to change, and you should contact the NBPTS.</u>

13. When will renewal submissions be evaluated?

The evaluation of the *Profile of Professional Growth* is expected to take place in July each year.

14. When will evaluation results be reported?

You should receive notification of a decision by October/November of the year in which you submit the *Profile of Professional Growth.*

15. How long will a renewal certificate be valid?

The original certificate is extended for ten years from the date of expiration.

16. What if I am teaching in a different field than I originally certified in? What if I am no longer actively teaching? Can I still attempt certificate renewal?

Yes. However, because Renewal requires classroom teaching in the area of your original certificate, you will need to establish a relationship and work with students of a colleague as part of the renewal process.

17. Can I attempt renewal after my certificate expires?

No. If you do not successfully complete the renewal process prior to the expiration of your certificate, you will need to apply and go through the National Board Certification process as a first-time candidate.

Final thoughts on Renewal...

Certification Renewal seems to have a much higher 'pass' rate than the original certification. (Estimates are 85-90 %.) It is less complex but very thorough. The release and inventory forms, detailed packing instructions, and writing requirement guidelines will be very familiar to you. As always, remember to go through the Standards book and highlight terms appearing repeatedly.

Use the NBPTS vocabulary! In doing this myself, I might suggest you get to know and use the following nomenclature as often as feasible:

- ✓ *Application* (of professional growth; to the real world in your teaching)

- ✓ *Collegial* (your working with other educators, parents, the community)

- ✓ *Contribution* (what you've given to the field of education)

- ✓ *Current, relevant, meaningful* (the information you teach and your growth professionally)

- ✓ *Demonstrate/cite* (evidence for student learning, and whatever else you are presenting)

- ✓ *Diversity, access, equity* (the fairness by which you run your classroom)

- ✓ *Evolvement; refined; deepened; sharpened* (how you have grown as an educator)

- ✓ *Impact* (on student learning, the field of education, parental involvement, etc.)

- ✓ *Ongoing, continual commitment* (that's what the NBPTS is looking for.)

- ✓ *Since certification* (to make evident that your professional growth were in the years since)

Appendix

Chapter 3

Worktable #3: Recognizing the Three types of writing

1. *Analytical*
2. *Reflective*
3. *Analytical*
4. *Descriptive*
5. *Analytical*
6. *Reflective*
7. *Descriptive*
8. *Analytical*
9. *Reflective*
10. *Descriptive*
11. *Analytical*
12. *Descriptive*
13. *Reflective*
14. *Analytical*
15. *Reflective*
16. *Descriptive*
17. *Analytical*
18. *Analytical*
19. *Reflective*
20. *Reflective*
21. *Descriptive*
22. *Descriptive*
23. *Analytical*
24. *Reflective*
25. *Reflective*
26. *Descriptive*
27. *Descriptive*
28. *Reflective*
29. *Analytical*
30. *Analytical*
31. *Descriptive*

Chapter 3

Scenarios analyses:

Note the italicized terms. Compare your analysis with this one.

Scenario 1

1. *Teacher*-focused, not student-centered.
2. *No* specificity—describe the class.
3. No specificity—how *much* time? Why?
4. *No* specificity—*what* prompt?
5. *Teacher*-centered.
6. *What* movie? Why was it shown? How was it related?
7. Watched *when?* How was the movie contextually appropriate?
8. *Teacher*-focused.
9. *No* specificity—*How* did you know?
10. *Teacher*-centered. (*Lack* of specificity. What *were* the goals for Jeremy?)
11. *Teacher*-centered. *How* were you shown? Was there a rubric? Is this *all* you saw?
12. *Why* has he not learned? But has he shown *personal* growth/improvement?

13. *Generalization. What* would you do to help him achieve this?
14. *Teacher*-focused.
15. *Knowledge of students.* You haven't shown enough regarding Jeremy to *recognize* personal application.
16. *Generalization. How* did he get confused? *Why?* Could it be the *teacher* was misunderstood?
17. *Teacher*-centered. How *specifically* did you reassess? Did you just retest Jeremy?
18. *Generalization. How* did he show improvement? *Why?*
19. *Generalization.* Why *don't* you know? How *could* you know?
20. *Bias.* What does collaboration have to do with it? Behavior? Ability? Grouping?
21. *Generalization.* How *would* you know? Why *should* you know?
22. *Generalization.* What's the *evidence?* How *well* did they understand it? How *many* did?

23. *Unsupported* generalization. *Evidence?* (Seems to contradict you!)

24. *Unsupported* statement. How do you *know* Jeremy does? *(Knowledge of students).*

25. *How* did he misunderstand? His fault or yours? What did he say?

26. How do you *know* this? What did you use to *assess* him?

Scenario 2

1. Inclusive word. Not merely teacher-centered.

2. Specific *details* (time, focus, students).

3. Passive; sounds less teacher-centered.

4. *Specificity* of what was done.

5. *Specific* contextual information.

6. Passive—note students—not teacher, are referenced.

7. Establishment of *prior preparation* (contextual information). Note: *inclusivism.*

8. Rubric. Specific reference to *how assessment was made.* Note: *student involvement* in development.

9. *Specificity.* Also note, it is the work, not Jeremy, which was criticized.

10. *Teacher as learner.*

11. Knowledge of students; *specificity.*

12. Knowledge of students; *specificity.*

13. Knowledge of students. Teacher looks beyond test scores.

14. *Specificity.* Knowledge of students.

15. Knowledge of students.

16. Key words: 'for example'; *specificity* (cp. an attorney building a case)

17. Knowledge of students.

18. *Anticipation* and *goal-setting.*

19. Key word: 'evidenced'; *specificity.* Teacher's knowledge of students. *Perceptive* reasoning.

20. *Reassessment* and *personalized.*

21. *Specificity. Analysis.* Recognition that it was a *misunderstanding,* not lack of learning.

22. *Analysis* of misunderstanding.

23. *Specificity* of recognition in the revised assessment prompt.

24. *Evidence* Jeremy is getting it right.

25. *Evidence* (specific citation).

26. Teacher's knowledge of subject *and* knowledge of student's understanding.

27. Teacher as learner: *analysis (& reflection).*

28. *Reflection.* Specificity in next assignment.

Chapter 5

Entry 1 Writing Sample

1. *Knowledge of students.*

2. Key words! (evidence).

3. Teacher as collaborator.

4. Planning: scope & sequence.

5. Student accountability.

6. Specific Knowledge of students.

7. Specific supporting evidence.

8. Teacher assessment.

9. Teacher caring to check *(Knowledge of students).*

10. *Assessment*

11. *Specificity* (watch abbreviations).

12. *Multiple assessment.*

13. *Specificity of example.*

14. Teacher as *learner.*

15. *Goal setting & measurement.*

16. *Specific* supporting evidence.

17. Individualized personal attention.

18. Individualized Personal attention/*reassessment.*

19. Teacher as *learner.*

20. *Assessment*/teacher as *learner.*

21. Citation of evidence.

Chapter 6

Answers to pre-videotaping quiz:

1. **F.** It can be wherever you could normally conduct a class.

2. **F.** Reflect in your *writing.* Facilitate in your *video.*

3. **T.** Very important.

4. **T.** The *interaction* is a key component.

5. **F.** May help, but is not required.

6. **F.** Not *'suggested'*.

7. **F.** Your *analysis* and *reflection* is the key to the video.

8. **T.** Important.

9. **F.** It may be to *you,* but not to the assessor.

10. **T.** In the instructions.

11. **F.** *Nothing* will substitute for weak addressing of the standards!

12. **T.** *Peer interaction* is important—especially in the group video.

13. **T.** Can't edit.

14. **F.** Takes up space in your writing, but a nice inclusion if some students can't be heard well.

15. **F.** It's how you *analyze* and *reflect* that counts.

16. **T.** Comfortable students will do better.

17. **T.** A fresh set of eyes always helps.

18. **T.** It's how you *analyze* and *reflect* on your <u>typical</u> teacher experiences that count.

19. **F.** Allow students to settle in.

20. **T.** Make sure what you want them to see is within the time limit.

21. **F.** Do it—just in case things get lost in transit.

22. **T.** The video should *describe.* You should *analyze* and *reflect.*

23. **T.**

24. **F.**

25. **F.**

Chapter 7

Documented Accomplishment: Entry 4 quiz answers

1. **T.** They show *interaction with parents/community.*

2. **F.** The key is *impact on student learning.*

3. **F.** One is fine. Remember, you can't include several from the same person.

4. **T.** *Never forget this.*

5. **F.** But one is a good idea.

6. **T.** Less is more in Entry 4!

7. **T.** But be sure they are *continual, interactive*, and *denote progress.*

8. **F.** Generally, these are not good unless they are truly exceptional.

9. **F.** It must be within the last year.

10. **T.** But make sure they show significant *improvement.*

11. **F.** Just make sure you relate *impact on student learning.*

12. **T.** Show *progression* in your growth as learner.

13. **F.** Entry 4 counts a bit less.

14. **T.** But it can be something *begun* (and continued) before the 5 years.

15. **T.** Make sure you document all three areas.

89

Bibliography and References

Much helpful information was collected *from the National Board Certification Candidate Resource Center.*

Other source material includes:

Daniels, Harvey and Bizar, Marilyn (1998). **Methods that Matter; Six Structures for Best Practice Classrooms**, Stenhouse

Einhorn, Carole. *"Enhanced Architecture of Accomplished Teaching"*, National Board Resource Center, Illinois State University. 2002.

Fitzpatrick, Kathleen A. (1998). **Indicators of School Quality—Vol. 1: Schoolwide Indicators of Quality, a Research-based Self-assessment Guide for Schools Committed to Continuous Improvement**, National Study of School Evaluation, 1699 East Woodfield Road, Suite 406, Schaumburg, IL 60173

Fletcher, Ralph (1996). **A Writer's Notebook; Unlocking the Writer Within You**, Avon Camelot Publishers

Gabriel, John G. (2005). **How to Thrive as a Teacher Leader**, ASCD

Glickman, Carl D. (2002). Leadership for **Learning; How to Help Teachers Succeed**, ASCD,

Harvey, Stephanie and Goudvis, Anne (2000) **Strategies That Work**, Stenhouse Publishers

Hines, Lynn; Miller, Brenda; Wright, Carol (2003). **A Toolkit for Success**, Western Kentucky University Research Foundation

Marzano, Robert J., Pickering, Debra J., and Pollack, Jane E. (2001). **Classroom Instruction that Works: Research-based Strategies for Increasing Student Achievement**, ASCD

Parks, Jerry L. (2004). **So, You Want to Become a National Board Certified Teacher?**, iUniverse

Parks, Jerry L. (2006). **Mentoring the *NBPTS* Candidate: A Facilitator's Guide,** iUniverse

Payne, Ruby K., Ph.D. (2001). **A Framework for Understanding Poverty**. Aha! Process, Inc.

Pratt, David (1997). **Terrific Teaching: 100 Great Teachers Share Their Best Ideas**, Pembroke Publishers Limited

Silver, Harvey F.; Strong, Richard W.; and Perini, Matthew (2000). **So Each May Learn; Integrated Learning Styles and Multiple Intelligences**, ASCD

Stronge, James H. (2002). **Qualities of Effective Teachers**, ASCD

Wong, Harry K. and Wong, Rosemary T. (1998). **The First Days of School: How to Be An Effective Teacher**, Harry Wong Publications

Made in the USA
San Bernardino, CA
12 October 2015